# Charles Slagle

**Destiny Image Publishers**
**P.O. Box 351**
**Shippensburg, PA 17257**

**"We Publish the Prophets"**

ISBN 0-914903-82-9

For Worldwide Distribution
Printed in the U.S.A.

First Printing: 1989
Second Printing: 1990
Third Printing: 1990
Fourth Printing: 1991
Fifth Printing: 1992
Sixth Printing: 1992
Seventh Printing: 1993
Eighth Printing: 1994
Ninth Printing: 1994
Tenth Printing: 1994

Destiny Image books are available through these fine distributors outside the United States:

Christian Growth, Inc.
Jalan Kilang-Timor, Singapore 0315

Lifestream
Nottingham, England

Rhema Ministries Trading
Randburg, South Africa

Salvation Book Centre
Petaling, Jaya, Malaysia

Successful Christian Living
Capetown, Rep. of South Africa

Vision Resources
Ponsonby, Auckland, New Zealand

WA Buchanan Company
Geebung, Queensland, Australia

Word Alive
Niverville, Manitoba, Canada

Inside the U.S., call toll free to order:
**1-800-722-6774**

# Dedication

This book is dedicated to three men who have profoundly influenced my perception of fatherhood—Dow Slagle, Gene Barnett and Hal Sacks.

I have deepest gratitude for the faithfulness, dedication, loving sacrifice and thirst after God that my earthly father, Dow Slagle (now residing with our Real Dad) bequeathed to me as a heritage. Through him, my foundation for faith was laid.

Gene Barnett, among all men yet living, most exhibits the kindness, the wit and the wisdom, and the heart of integrity and innate goodness one desires to see in fatherhood. Truly, this man exemplifies the role of father as friend.

Hal Sacks, though my own peer, lifted the veil from my heart that blocked my view of my heavenly Father's desire to receive me, and through Hal's ministry my spirit gained desire to live. May our Father richly reward him.

Because of these valiant men and their influence upon my life, my soul has been liberated so that it might soar to the heights and embrace the heart of God...the *best* Dad that ever was, is, or ever shall be.

# Acknowledgments

Before I render thanks to all others who have helped me, I wish from my heart to honor and recognize our heavenly Father. But for Him, there would be no book to write, no thoughts to share, no hope to give, no life to live and words would mean nothing at all. Holy, majestic, just, pure and tender; our Father is all of these things — and more. He is my *Dad*. My Strong Dad. My *Real* Dad. And all because of Jesus Christ, implanted in the womb of Mary by the Holy Spirit 2,000 years ago. It was then that The Word became flesh and dwelt among us. The Son of God was literally *translated* into the Son of *Man*.

When God grew up in our midst, He emerged as a Shepherd, a Deliverer, a Life-Giver and a perfect Mirror-Reflection of His Father. His whole purpose in visiting our world was to restore *us* to commune with Father. And that He did, but it cost Him His life to do it. He wooed us away from our death march into hell by showing us His Father's face — His essence and His character. The scene of the crucifixion is the most passionate portrayal of God's heart ever beheld in any time or any world — Perfect Love, dying at the hands of His own creatures. For only in light of the cross can we ever see clearly what our Father in heaven is like.

Why did it take me thirty-nine years to see this? I don't know. I was reared in a Christian environment. All I know is that when this basic revelation came alive in my spirit, it utterly transformed my whole perception of God the Father and my relationship with Him. Now we are friends. And it goes without saying — I owe all that I have and all that I am to Him.

However, our Father has selected many other of His "daring disciples" to assist in compiling this book. I would not disappoint Him by neglecting to give them worthy mention. Without their help, this book would be filled with hopeless discrepancies, *exceeding* deep mysteries, countless theological abstractions and a host of grammatical absurdities. And nobody could make head or tails of its purpose!

Like the cover and illustrations? Cliff Hawley did the artwork! His artistic ability is surpassed only by his noble spirit. Our dear friends, Deborah Holtzclaw and Sherry Spoontz, (professionally known as Charash Design) provided that wonderful script for the title and donated many hours to otherwise help us. Journalist Elaine Goode and Professor Miriam Reinhold, both English majors and mighty women of valor, wielded their red and green pens with rare skill. They deserve notable honor and many thanks from us all in that they preserved the English language from utter destruction. Truly!

I owe the concept of these "letters" to Carolyn Barnett, who sent the first letter from "Dad" I ever received — written prophetically by her very own hand. Thank God for her ministry! Much of the homework that had to be done for this project was done by our beloved office manager, Jayne Hartong. I know no one on earth with a purer servant's heart. May God reward her for unscrambling my scribbles and for translating, typing and retyping them countless times. And what more can I say? Evelyn Guiher, Christine Noble and Onnie Roberts each imparted very vital input. Also, I am indebted to Norman and Grace Barnes, Judson Cornwall, Brian and Pam Richardson, Yvonne Sanchez and Jerry Schroeder for their encouragement, input and contributions. These dear friends truly gave of themselves as unto the Lord. May He richly reward them.

In addition, I would like to mention two other very special people: my beloved son, Bryan Paul, who taught me how to be a dad, and my wife Paula. Paula has tirelessly edited and typed. But most of all, she has kept all of this work in a good semblance of order, yea, despite my talent to clutter. But it is not just what she has done. It is who and what she has been to me. Were it not for Paula's loyalty, love and sacrifice, I am sure this book would not have been written — at least, not by this guy. My eyes to see Father were healed by her faith, and I am not ashamed to admit it. Paula and I are one. Therefore, any revelation or blessing which may proceed out of me proceeds from my lovely "counterpart" as well.

May our Father bless all who have contributed to this project in any way or to any degree.

# Author's Note

Several distinctives will easily be seen by all who read this book. They are the following:

(1) Because many of the letters touch on more than one issue, they are not divided into chapter-like categories. These messages are intended to unveil various aspects of the Father's heart. They were not meant to be collections compiling a reference book for "problem solving" or to replace the "promise box." However, they are listed by titles to help the reader find his way.

(2) The portrayal of Father's wit, irony and humor is shown abundantly in the Bible but, unfortunately, is seldom portrayed in other writings. This I am prayerfully attempting to rectify to some small degree. (See Num. 22:28; I Sam. 5-6; Prov. 17:14; Matt. 11:16-19, 23:24.)

(3) The letters are often addressed to "deliverers," "saviors," "conquerors," "liberators" and "freedom fighters." This is to remind the reader that our Dad takes seriously His call for the body of Christ to continue the work of Jesus in the world. As Christ was in this world, so are we. And as Christ was sent to this world, so are we. (See Obad. 1:21; John 20:21; I John 4:17.)

(4) In seeking to motivate the reader to righteous choices, the letters appeal more to reason and good sense than to fear of coming judgment. Hence, the reader may find phrases that sound a little odd (coming from God) cropping up. "In My view," "I think" and "the way I see it" are examples of this. This is to show that our Dad is always seeking to help us view things as He views them — to see as He sees. He knows that when we begin to see as He sees, think as He thinks and feel as He feels, we will find ourselves strongly motivated to act as He acts. The

Scriptures tell us to copy (emulate and mimic) our heavenly Father as His dearly beloved children. (See Is. 1:18; Eph. 5:1; Col. 1:9,10.)

(5) The reader will note that many of the letters are signed "Dad." This is what "Abba, Father" literally does mean in the scriptures. The Bible clearly teaches us that Father God longs to relate to each of His children on intimate, family terms. (See Rom. 8:15-17.)

(6) The capitalization of pronouns (Us, We, Our, Ours) which include the Divine Person with the reader is a respectful and affectionate reference to the reader's royal status as Father's child. Our Father longs to elevate our viewpoint concerning our relationship with Him.

On the other hand, all references to satan are purposely not capitalized unless they occur at the beginning of a sentence. By this, I am seeking to contrast the diminished power and significance of our enemy against the might and authority of our God and His children. (See Isa. 14:12-16; Rom. 8:15-17; Eph. 1:15-23; I Pet. 2:9,10.)

(7) The verb form "I AM" is consistently capitalized when spoken by Father. This is the name of our God and it is emphasized to remind the reader of His unchanging love, power and faithfulness. (See Ex. 3:13,14.)

The messages which have now become the body of this book began as a series of "letters" from Father to me. In time, as these personal letters began to accumulate, I became sensitive that our Lord desired that I share them with others.

**Only the Bible is infallibly inspired by God.** The messages in this book are not prophecies, per se. I am fully aware that our Father may choose to give them a personal, prophetic impact to some readers on occasion, but no special inspiration is claimed. However, I pray that the words of this book will prove helpful for other "weary warriors" who seek to increasingly know our Father's heart. Obviously, these messages are intended to comfort the reader with the same comforts by which we, the Slagles have also been comforted. (See II Cor. 1:3-7.)

# Foreword

You hold in your hands an unusual book; but who would expect the Slagles to do the ordinary? *From the Father's Heart* could have been written only by one who has walked at length with God through times pleasant and times painful; for experiential knowledge, such as this book offers, comes no other way.

The literary style would suggest that these are a series of prophecies, but no such claim has been made. These are the meditations of one whose knowledge of God has broken the boundaries of religion and has released him into a fresh walk with a believable Person Who calls Himself "Father." It is not written in the abstract, nor is the safety of the third person used. This book speaks the message about God as though He were the speaker. It comes from His lips to our hearts.

I recommend against reading the book in one sitting. Savor it; contemplate its message, and react to what you read. This book is far more than information given; it is inspiration shared. You will not read many pages before you find yourself being personally addressed. Sit there awhile and meditate. You have more time left in your life than you believe, so don't rush through these pages.

Reading this manuscript prior to its publication proved to be a source of blessing and inspiration to me. I am thrilled to see another whose concepts of God have broadened without becoming unduly religious. Sameness so often becomes staleness. The different approach taken in this book tends to make even the familiar fresh.

The days that loom before us demand that we know our God. Daniel, looking down the pages of history to the end of time, declared: "... the people who know their God shall be strong, and carry out great exploits" (Dan. 11:32).

Perhaps we know much *about* God without actually *knowing* God Himself. It is now time for modern Christians to come to actually *know* Him. To whatever end this book helps believers achieve that intimate knowledge of God, it will be an invaluable blessing.

Judson Cornwall, Th.D

# Introduction

About halfway through the writing of what now comprises this book, a dear friend of ours pulled me aside after spending a few days at our home. She said to me, "Paula, that's not the same Charles Slagle I knew a few years ago!" She and Charles had sat up half the night before — Charles reading to her excerpts from this book, discussing the things he was learning and new aspects he was discovering about Father God, his heavenly Dad. She said to me that morning, "He's changed, he's different."

As she and I talked, I began to realize, yes, Charles had changed. Over the years I'd watched as a new and sovereign prophetic anointing had thrust him into graphic and specific ministry to individuals, not only in our church meetings but often in the marketplace as well. And yet I'd heard him question...if God could give him such accurate and detailed information to minister to others, why would He not speak to him personally in the same way? There was always that sense of unworthiness, which is universal to all of us, and the fear of being led astray by his own mind that stood in the way of such a relationship. Too, there was a very fractured and cloudy concept of God's fatherhood that needed correction.

In many areas of Charles' life the enemy had worked to build misconceptions and fears about his heavenly Father — fears that, no matter how hard he tried, he'd never make it. He feared that, at the end of the day, God would bring to his attention things he'd totally overlooked — sins, shortcomings and failures that he could and would have asked forgiveness for, had he only known! Charles had yet to realize that God was his ally, not his adversary.

Around the time of his natural father's death, Charles shared some of these fears and questions with a beloved friend and Spirit-led counselor, Carolyn Barnett. She suggested he begin "conversing" with God — spending time with Him, asking all his questions, expressing whatever was on his heart. She encouraged him to "listen" and to write down the answers he thought he was receiving. Little did any of us realize what would come from his time with his Father.

Before long, his constant companions had become a yellow legal pad, a pen, a Bible and a thesaurus! As the scribbles on his paper began to grow into a series of "letters" from God, Charles began to realize he was getting a glimpse of God that revealed Him as the loving heavenly Father he'd always sought. The letters were words of correction, encouragement, exhortation, understanding, compassion, teaching. Most often they were messages directly from the heart of Father God to Charles himself. But over the months, as we began to share them in our meetings, we'd watch the Holy Spirit touch the hearts of others, using those very same words that had ministered to Charles. We began to realize that these letters were an implement that could acquaint many, many people with the personality and character of Father God and, hopefully, inspire them to seek an intimate father/child relationship with Him. And how better to touch an even greater number of lives than a book? Hence, what you hold in your hands.

I would encourage you to read these letters aloud. Use both your physical eyes and ears. Together, these two senses will be avenues to help the words of this book reach your heart. But more importantly, listen and see with the eyes and ears of your spirit (See Matt. 13:16). As you read, give the Holy Spirit opportunity to reveal the true heart of your heavenly Father and to cause your spirit-man to begin to know — experience and embrace — the Father of all creation.

Yes, Charles Slagle has changed and is continuing to change, largely as a result of hearing and receiving from his heavenly Dad in the process of writing this book. I've watched these letters from the Father's heart — these revelations of God's nature and ways — heal Charles' own heart. And I know the same can happen for you.

Paula Slagle

from the Father's Heart

*ON YOUR SIDE*
Ps. 121; Zeph. 3:17; Rom. 8:31-39

hild,

If anyone wants you to succeed, I do. If anyone is on your side, I AM. There is no one more committed to your happiness than I, and no one even begins to love you like I do. And I want to clarify something. My love for you is more — far more — than a patronizing concern for your welfare. I like you. I *enjoy* you.

I realize you find all this hard to believe, but I want you to believe it. You'll have to sooner or later, so why not now? I think about you all the time, and I will stop at nothing to remind you of My presence. Haven't you noticed?

Entreatingly,
Dad

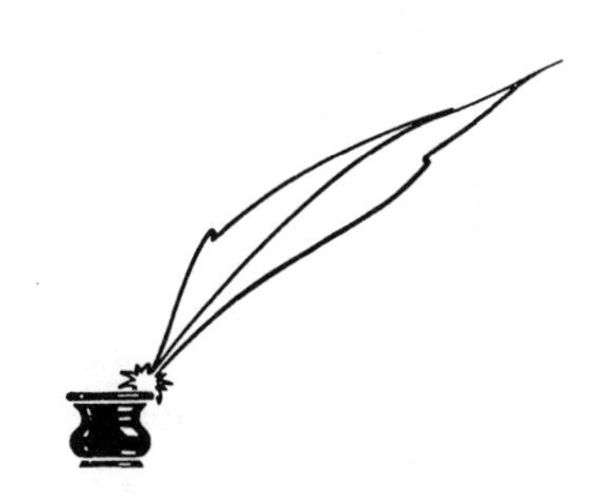

*SELF-MANAGEMENT*
II Tim. 1:7

Struggling Deliverer,

Next time, begin the day with authority. I gave you not a spirit of fear, but a spirit of love, power and of self-management. Begin to act like it! Decide to keep a sense of humor. Laugh at all mistakes, interruptions and obstacles, and stop worrying about your ignorance.

Has it not occurred to you that I AM in charge of your ignorance as well as your knowledge? Think! Has your mouth not uttered deeper wisdom than you dreamed possible when you have simply "been yourself," while oblivious to the tensions — the issues around you? A man ignorant of all the rules can be a miracle-worker, and the knowledge of too many problems can create a prison. Remember, all knowledge is Mine and all ignorance is Mine. And you are Mine. Live in the joy of that fact.

Always,
Father

## *FIRST THINGS FIRST*

Isa. 32

Devoted Disciple,

As I have promised, you *will* see the King reigning in glory! You will recognize the true reign of Christ in His Church when His chosen ones no longer strive and quibble about words, but walk in the power of Kingdom love. When the world can look to a member of Our household as a mighty rock providing cool shade and protection, or as a stream springing forth in a parched desert, the reign of My Son will then be self-evident — obviously obvious and undeniably undeniable.

Now do you see why I have been allowing you these opportunities to show patience and forgiveness? I have been answering your prayers. Do you not remember? I do. You have repeatedly prayed for love, unity and cooperation among the members of Our house, and, naturally, I have begun the work in you. As you are discovering, no one is more dedicated to the principle of "first things first" than I ...

Be of good cheer, for despite your doubts, you are progressing better than you think. And be comforted in the knowledge that your brothers and sisters are undergoing the very same training throughout the world. As I have told you, the Church and the world are on the brink of an unprecedented wave of My glory and power. At present, I AM making you ready as My chosen redeemer, along with many others. In the meantime, will you be patient with yourself? With them? And with Me? I AM!

Dad

*REAL JOY*
Gal. 5:22,23

Fretful Freedom Fighter,

Shall I tell you about real joy? Joy begins by knowing Me and then is multiplied by taking an interest in people — not things, conditions or acquisitions. And happiness never just happens. No, happiness is a result — a by-product. One feels it by receiving My love and joy, and then giving them away. Happiness is a choice. A man or a woman must *decide* to be happy — now. Has it ever come to your mind that most unhappiness stems from ingratitude and failure to take pleasure in the gifts one already has?

Child, when will you learn to joy in the midst of all circumstances? If they be hard, delightful, or perhaps just suddenly different — lay hold of contentment and take joy as My gift! It *is* My gift, for contentment comes not by external conditions — it is the fruit of exercising confidence in Me.

Again, happiness is a choice! So, in a very important sense, to choose happiness is to choose heaven. Will you choose it now? *Be* happy! Find reasons to rejoice and make opportunities to relieve the sufferings of others. Learn to be content in every circumstance — including this present one. Decide and begin now to practice continual praise! Your joy will overflow, I promise.

By the way, you are obviously right about one thing...I have not answered some of your prayers, for I have deliberately ignored your pleas that I shorten your earthly days and immediately transfer you to heaven. And you should be grateful that I have. Honestly, child. You had no idea what you were asking. I mean, in your recent frame of mind your presence here would hardly have proven a blessing to you — or to any of the rest of Us, for that matter!

Truly but Tenderly,
Dad

*LITTLE STEPS*
Zech. 4:10

Delightful Deliverer!

You are not wrong to be stepping out in faith at the moment. Am I not the One who released you into this path by My very own words? Just remember not to judge by outward appearances. Also, refuse to retreat into doubt and introspection when some of those little steps you are taking seem to fall short of shaking heaven and earth. Bear in mind — it is first the seed and the sprout, then the stalk and the foliage, and finally the flower and the fruit.

Son, Our Kingdom is an enduring one. It is built on a Solid Foundation — line upon line, precept upon precept — here a little, there a little. Our Kingdom is a quiet one, but an invincible one. Is it noise and fireworks you want, or power?

I have spoken these thoughts to your heart already, but I knew you would enjoy having them confirmed...Keep moving! I AM!

Proudly! Joyfully!
Dad

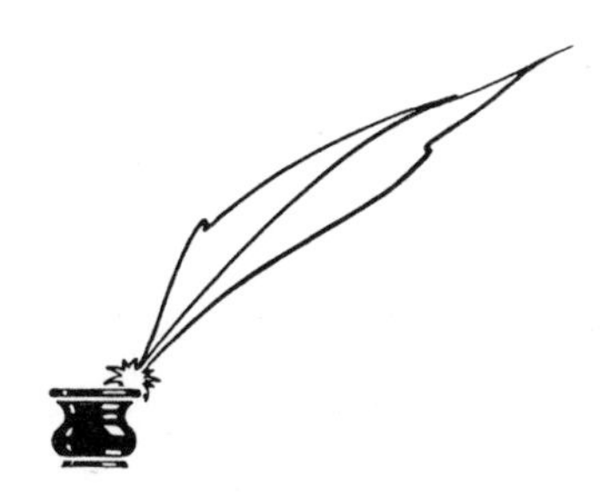

*TRUST IS A MUST*
II Tim. 1:12

Fearful One,

You have My Word; what else do you need? Have I ever betrayed or forsaken you? Did Jesus not promise, "...he who comes to Me, I will in no wise cast out"? Then you must choose to remember His promise and decide to forget your doubts. Now — more than ever — trust is a must. So will you forsake those fears and refuse to heed outward appearances? Sooner or later you must, for despite your doubts or those of anyone else, I AM at work to fulfill My words.

Trust Me now! If you will, this test need not come again. These things were allowed, not to decrease your faith, but to enlarge it. I AM answering your prayers that I enlarge your heart to contain greater faith. And I have used the debased and the weak to do it — even the frailty of your own flesh.

Never fear, I will keep every promise. Meanwhile, will you trust My integrity to hold you up by grace? That kind of trust builds the foundation for all victories to follow, and it is the only commitment I ask of you. I will fulfill My commitment; but now I AM enabling you to see that, by My grace, you also can fulfill yours. Trust Me. Can you think of a better plan of action? Not if it's *My* power you want.

Forever!
Dad

Will you
trust my
integrity
to hold
you up
by grace?

## *SPECIAL EFFECTS*

I Kings 19:11,12; Matt. 13:16,17

ruth Seeker,

It is just not My style to thunder from heaven with a booming voice accompanied by the special effects of wind and fire — at least not in ordinary circumstances. No, I have purposely planned to speak softly so those who truly desire to hear My voice will hear it — but only those. Furthermore, it is not My nature to intrude where I AM not wanted! And being the very Author of protocol and propriety, I seldom have done so, except in rare moments when expediency required it for the sake of all. Besides (though some will never believe it), I usually prefer a more natural approach to the supernatural.

I do speak, and I speak more often than you imagine, but all who desire to hear Me must *will* to hear Me. All have spiritual ears. I have seen to that. Unfortunately, very few in your world even think about them, let alone exercise their wills to use them! Do you remember that Jesus said of the clergy of His day, "they have ears, but *will* not hear with them"? Child, hearing is a choice! It is just that simple.

If a man desires to hear My voice, he must choose, will and decide to listen to his heart. Then he must choose, will and decide to act upon those quiet thoughts He believes I AM speaking. He must trust My integrity enough to respond to My leading — knowing he *cannot* be given a spirit of error to lead him astray when he has asked that I give him My Spirit to guide him. Such a man will do the works of Jesus, for he will refuse to yield to the clamor of his emotions, the fear of failure, or the fear of man. He will walk by the hearing of faith. And the result? He will walk like a son of God.

Are you thirsty? Are you yearning to join the adventure? Then come! Come drink! Drink of the Waters of Life freely! The Well of My Unconquerable Life *is* surging within you! Christ has become your knowledge and wisdom, for He dwells in you, and He *is* the *Voice* of My Word! *Listen*, and your soul *shall* live — forever!

I Promise,
Father

## *I HAVE NOT BETRAYED YOU*

I Pet. 2:20-23

Broken One,

I have not betrayed you. Mortals have, I know. But may I share a secret with you? At this very moment — even now — you hold great power either of life or death, sorrow or loss in your hands. I AM not often angry, yet today I AM for the pain they willfully caused you.

Thank you for allowing Me to defend your interests! I AM happy you asked Me to do so. Yes, vengeance is Mine! I *will* repay. So what would you have Me to do? Search your heart, and do consider very carefully, for what is done cannot be undone, little one ...

Shall I judge them strictly by the ways they have dealt with you? Or shall I consider all preceding factors — their shattered hopes, their inner struggles — even as I have done for you? And what if they repent? You decide. I await your answer patiently, sorrowfully, and with deepest compassion.

Tenderly,
Dad

P.S. I trust you. Remember, mercy triumphs over judgment!

## *LAUGH AT THE THREATS*

Ps. 34:1-10

old Pioneer!

You have come this far, so what makes you think you will fall short of the goal now? Have you been listening to all those "wise reasoners" again? You know — those who delight in foreseeing problems, criticizing failures and freely voicing their opinions while dwelling in the comfortable safety of theory, unbelief and inactivity?

Words, words, and *more* worthless words! When will you finally decide to believe in the gifts I placed within you and choose to laugh at all those silly reasonings?

If it is safety you want, then you will do far better to listen to Me and follow your heart. Has experience not taught you this? Besides, pioneers like Ourselves have always seen safety in a different light than those who try to make a career out of it; don't you agree? Laugh at the threats, son. Laugh and get on with *enjoying* your life! I do. Follow your heart and follow your dream! I AM with you, so what else do you think you will ever need? A few more prophets of gloom and doom? Not on your life! And *certainly* not on Mine.

Still Chuckling...
Dad

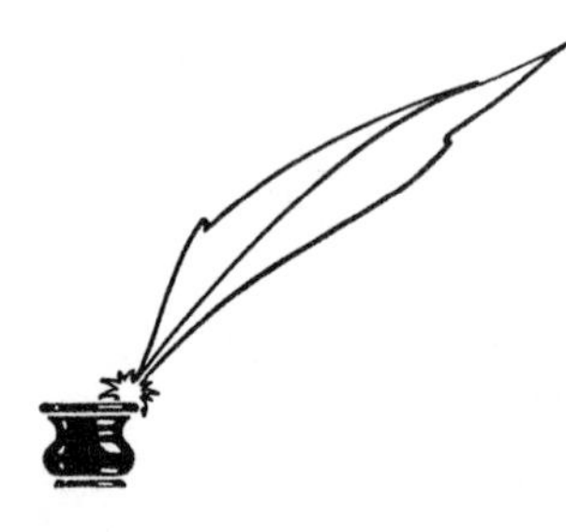

*OUR SONG*
Ps. 34:8; Ps. 100; Zeph. 3:17

Weary One,

When I ask you to sing praises and to delight in Me from your heart, please bear in mind — I AM not seeking your encouragement. Since when did Everlasting Strength need encouragement? Or anything else for that matter?

My command to give praise is a *love* command. I AM inviting you to join The Dance — the Cosmic Celebration of Joy! There and there alone can you learn the Song of songs. And there only can you also hear the song I have sung over you since you were born.

Enter My courts! Come into them — with praise! Praise is the gateway to My throne room. So praise, child! Enter in by praise! I AM drawing you into the melody all heaven has been singing since before time began. We have a glorious song to sing, you and I, and the tedious drone of earth-songs will disappear in the splendor of Ours, I assure you.

And when you sing Our song, hurting one, Our hearts will harmonize as one. In the glory of that union all else will harmonize as well. But you must sing the Song of praise if ever you would see...

Your Father

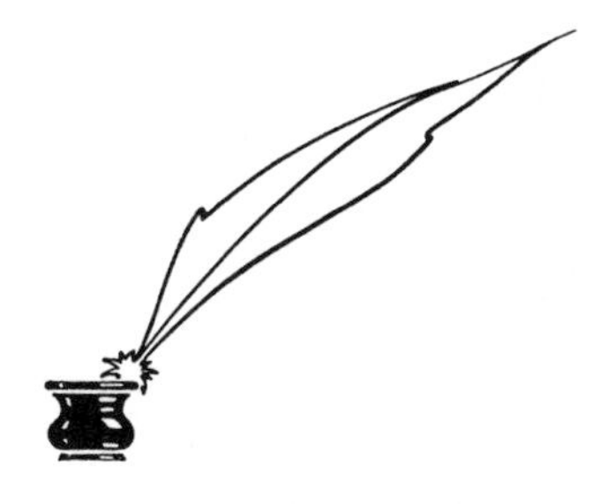

*COMPARISON*
Ps. 139; II Cor. 10:12,13; I Pet. 2:4-9

Chosen Conqueror,

Comparison is simply asking for depression. No one is "equal" to anyone else because I have created the human family in such a way as to engender mutual need and a supportive sharing among its members. You may as well learn to live with this fact: you will never be equal to your friends or even your enemies, because I never intended that you be.

Frankly, the whole idea of equality is a fallacy, for no real person ever could or ever should be an exact replica of another. If I had wanted tin soldiers, could I not have made them easily enough? But if I had, your very capacity to recognize inequality would not exist. You would not be a person at all, but only a copy and a caricature of a concept, without the ability to be truly happy or unhappy. The "you" that now thinks to question My fairness would not even be. Has it never occurred to you that all sameness is equal — but equal to nothingness? To reduce all to the identical is to erase all potential for personhood and merely to arrange a new form of the trivial at best, and nothingness at worst. Is this the fate you would assign to yourself? Or all others?

Child, no two people can ever be equally interesting, conversant, intelligent, talented or strong, for all have different needs and all have different gifts. And why? Because all were made to fit together as living stones comprising My Holy Temple — some large, some small, some short, some tall, some hard, some soft — but all for the glory of all.

Can you now see the futility of envy? Child, you have not because you ask not. Ask! I will complete you, but by association, not duplication. And believe it or not, I have also desired to complete others by introducing them to you! You do have many strengths you have forgotten in the midst of all your comparisons. So why not think of someone else for a change? If you will, I believe you will find yourself even liking yourself — in spite of yourself!

Patiently,
Dad

P.S. Remember, to complain and compare is to live in despair. How could one man's weakness ever rival another man's strength? It's as logical as two plus two equals five!

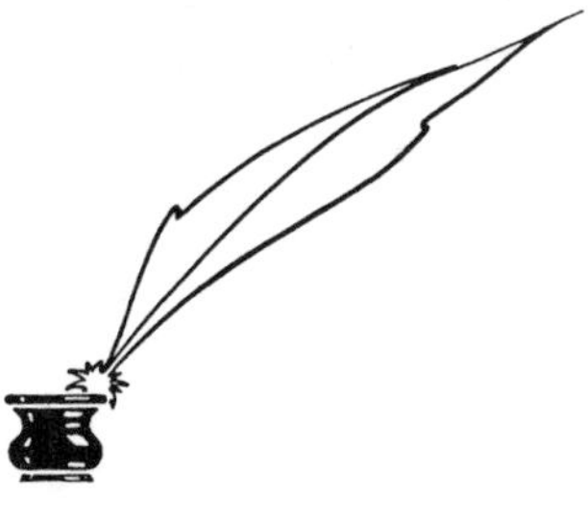

### *I SEE ALL*

Rom. 8:28; Rom. 11:33-36

Diligent Disciple,

I AM not ashamed of you. You have embarrassed yourself, but you have not embarrassed Me. Not in the least.

I give you time to learn and space to grow because, as a wise Father, I know your welfare depends on your having actual knowledge, born of experience. Those who speak otherwise — saying My holiness demands instant perfection and flawless performance — know nothing of fatherhood and misrepresent Me in their ignorance.

My ways are not the ways of men. I AM not one to worry about outward appearances, and neither do I fret over the blunders of My children. I look at the heart. Don't you remember? I see *all.* In fact, I can see no other way. All is all I ever see. So how can One who sees everything at all times *ever* worry about anything at any time?

I thought you'd enjoy the reminder...

Love,
Dad

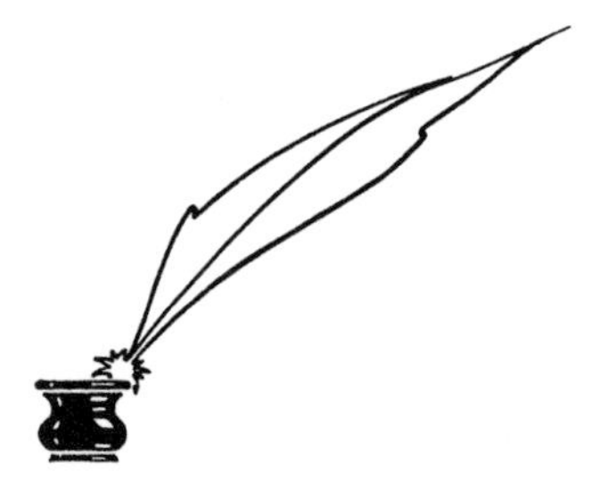

*SAFETY*
Dan. 11:32; Phil. 4:13

Son,

Being safe is hardly a worthwhile goal to seek. I mean, safety should be one of the very least concerns of a conqueror. How unlike you! Since when have you ever been one to worry about trying something different? So why are you beginning to play the cautious role at this stage of the game?

Shall I repeat some of your own advice to you? Come now! It was you who said, and you have said it repeatedly, "There is no safety apart from doing the Father's will." And again, you have also said, "The only thing that assures safety or protection of the truest quality is to follow Christ."

Son, you know I AM not one to nag or harass, so I will not belabor the point. But don't you think it's time to rid yourself of those ridiculous rehearsals for retreat? Repent! Let Us enjoy a good laugh together!

Dad

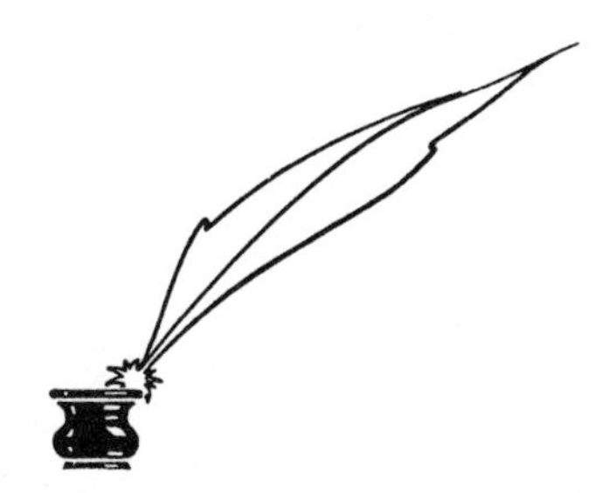

*FAVOR*
I Cor. 1:4-7; II Cor. 3:7-18

nxious One,

You do have favor. You have Mine. You are filled and surrounded with My glory! And although My glory may not always feel very glorious to your emotions or appear very glorious to your natural eyes, it abides with you nevertheless. It is an invisible shield; like any other shield, its worth is determined by what it does, not by how it appears.

Have I not recently shown you the power of My glory? I have. You know I have. I have granted you favor in the marketplace where you least expected it. I have opened doors no one else ever could have opened. I have protected you from losses you never could have foreseen given a million lifetimes. And gladly have I done it!

Child, I don't mind your having grown accustomed to My glory, and neither am I offended that you have learned to walk in it with hardly a thought of its presence. Would you expect your own children to be constantly thanking you for the roof over their heads or the clothes on their backs? Of course not!

And so it is with Me, little one. My glory is your *natural* inheritance! I was just wondering why you have been entertaining all those irrational fears lately — pleading for My protection and favor when you've had them all this time....

Tenderly,
Dad

*STRETCHES OF SILENCE*
I John 3:1,2

Delightful Son,

There is just no way to avoid some of those long stretches of "silence," as you call them. As your own experience has proven, My ways are higher than yours and My plans for you far exceed your ability to imagine.

What use is *information* to a man ravaged by the ache of physical need? Would giving him a course in human psychology or anatomy satisfy his hunger, quench his thirst, or relieve his pain? So it is with you, son. Now is a *feeding* time, a *building* time — not a time for words. When words are needed I will speak them; you know I always have.

For now, will you review those words I spoke to you earlier? If you will, I think you'll find your questions already answered. And never mind the apologies. You've not disillusioned Me. How could you? I never had any illusions.

And what makes you think I have "given up" on you? That nonsense never crosses My mind except when you bring it up yourself. Has it ever occurred to you how your even *thinking* I would cuts Me to the heart? Son, your reluctance to trust My integrity hurts far more than any sin arising from the weakness of your flesh.

One day when you truly know Me and realize how much I care for you, you will also discover My strength has swallowed up your weakness...

Forever in Joy!
Dad

### *I STOOD WITH YOU*

Ps. 3; Matt. 12:18-21

Little One,

Do you really believe I have burdened you with this inner conflict? Am I so cruel, so unreasonable? How could Love commit such an act? No, you know it isn't true. I AM the One who has been holding you, keeping you from utter despair in those hours you wept alone. I have seen your tears and I have known how you have yearned to please Me. I have cried with you, feeling the shame of your humiliation as if it were My own. And it was My own, little one, it was.

I have also noted the withdrawals and "righteous" judgments of those you trusted. Be assured, I saw it all. I have seen your desperate search for answers. When your pain drove you to share those secret sorrows of your heart, and they rewarded your trust with treachery, I stood with you. I know. They justified it all in My name and called it "honoring the Word" and "faithfulness to the cause of Christ," but may I tell you what I called it? I called it *disgusting.* Of all sins, from robbery to prostitution, I find none more revolting than sanctimony and hypocrisy. And there are certainly none more damnable.

Please ... Will you remember that if foolish men judge by the outward appearance, it is not so with Me? I see the inner wounds underlying those surface sins the hypocrites love to gossip about — truly I do. Have I ever been One to snuff out a smoldering wick or trample a man who is down? Come now! You know better. I AM the *Righteous* Judge.

So child, despite the failures of your friends or those I once trusted as shepherds of My flock, will you please keep trusting in Me? Will you forgive them so the weight of their sins may be lifted from your tired shoulders? Heaven knows you've carried burdens enough.

And don't give up. Few others have known or cared, but I know how long you have waited. Your deliverance is close, little one, very close indeed. *Rest in My love!* Believe Me, the joy of your freedom will banish all grief as death is swallowed up by life, and the old gives way to the new. There *is* no other way it could be. I AM forever committed.

Truly,
Dad

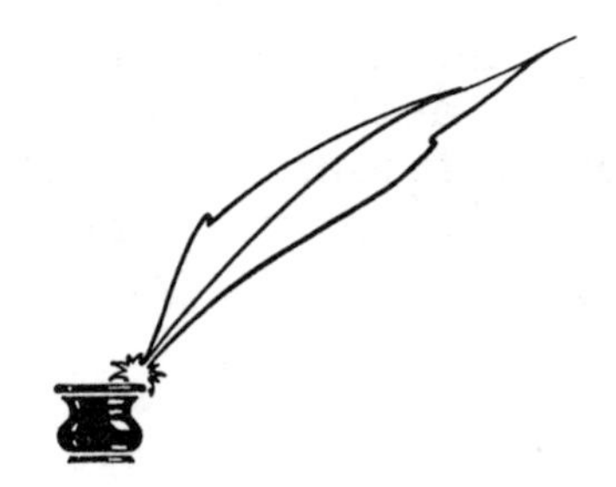

## *I SEE THE REAL YOU*

Rom. 5:17-19

iligent One,

Having done all you can do, refuse to take responsibility for the failures of others. Reject all temptation to introspect and stop analyzing your past. When I see you, I see you not as you were then, or even as you are now. No, I see the *real* you — the *glorious* you that, even now, I AM opening your own eyes to see!

Assuming guilt for the sins of others or for your own sins already forgiven only darkens the eyes of your spirit, tying you to problems not your own. Renounce the works of darkness! Refuse to rehearse their memories! Return to joy! I have all power and all things are in My control. Rejoice in My grace!

You need not worry about "using" My grace. As I have said before, if you were to become lax or careless about it, I would be the first to let you know. Grace alone has power to save, child! If you don't use it, what else in earth or heaven do you expect to use? Willpower!? Positive thinking!? HA! I'm laughing *with* you — honestly.

Love,
Dad

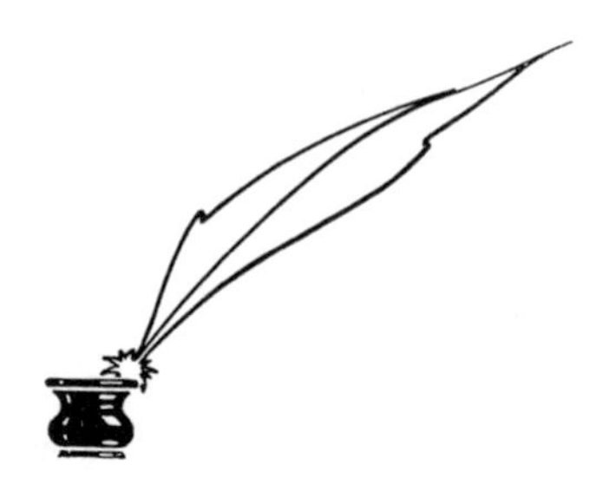

*LOOK AT THE PLAN*
Heb. 12

Fretful One,

Don't look at the pain. Look at the plan! Look at the purpose! Why do you equate discipline with punishment? Why should I *punish* you? You are the one doing the punishing, not I. Do you expect Me to help you worsen the wound? Sorry. You're looking in the wrong Department... If it's guilt and condemnation you want, you need to consult a good religionist — *there* is the place to look. But why not take My advice, have a good laugh and stay with the program?

Did you forget? I told you earlier that you would soon be in training for the big game of the season. Well, this is it! Rejoice and be glad! I *know* you. You can do it! By the way, have you had a good look at those muscles of yours lately? I have.

Proudly!
Dad

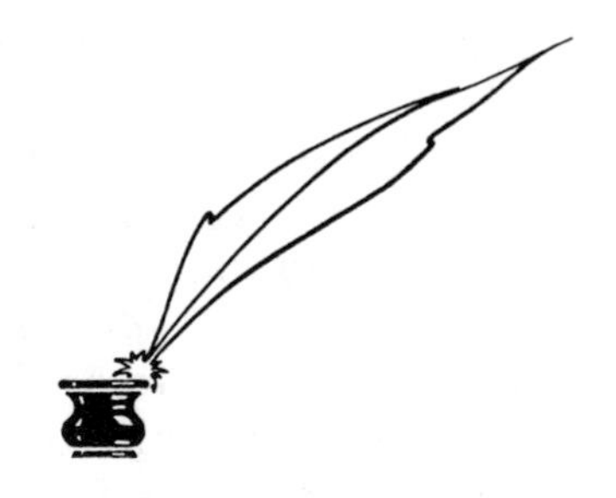

*GOOD COMPANY*
Heb. 5:8

Daring Deliverer,

But of course! Often you will be misunderstood! Was it not the same with Jesus? If you recall, My Son was constantly criticized for His unorthodox behavior.

When He was bold, His critics called Him proud, and when love compelled Him to heal the sick on the Sabbath, contrary to religious custom, they accused Him of sin. Jesus was the very personification of humility, yet even His humility was called hypocrisy. His acceptance of *all* men and women, without regard to their social standing, was considered an outrage! His opponents not only criticized it — they publicized it as immoral.

And your Lord stirred up controversy constantly, just by virtue of what He was! Some thought Him too strict, while others thought Him too lenient. Still others thought Him a rebel while many thought Him a pacifist. Do you recall how Jesus was often interrupted in the midst of His ministry? Rudely interrogated and mocked? I do. Yes, *Jesus,* the Perfect God-Man, was the Object of ridicule, controversy and gossip.

But He laughed the shame to scorn! And why? Jesus came to heal, not to please, and I received glory through His willing obedience. If He were unable to gratify all, then certainly you cannot.

Child, I know you're tired of the trivia, but how many times do you think Christ answered the same quibbling questions in a single day? Did men ever seek to use Him for their own selfish ends? How slow were His disciples to comprehend His message? How often did the Son of God find Himself settling silly squabbles among His followers? Did those who demanded His time value it? Did Jesus ever meet with suspicion, unrealistic expectations, or ingratitude? *Is the student greater than his Teacher?* You decide.

Your Master was the King of Kings, yet He made

Himself a Servant. His kind of ministry does demand His kind of cross. And child, it is merely your reasonable service. Remember, it is for the joy set before you. Joy, joy and more joy! *Multiplied* in this life and in the world to come! And, yes, with some persecutions — but why not? After all, you are in very Good Company...

With Deepest Understanding and Joy,<br>Dad

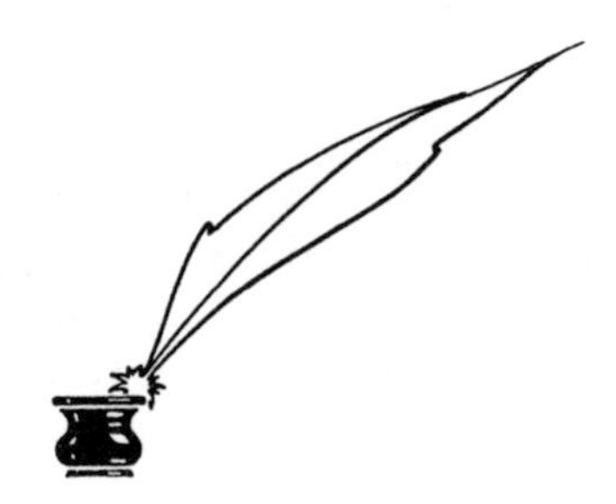

*ORDINARY THINGS*
Matt. 10:42; Matt. 25:40

on,

Has it ever come to your mind that I *like* ordinary things? Yes, the things you call ordinary are the very instruments I have chosen to use in your world, and I call them wonderful. They are just as miraculous as any other miracles I have — so please stop questioning your gifts, will you? Do We always have to be pulling rabbits out of hats?

What good is it to raise the dead and heal the sick if no one thinks to feed and clothe them after they have been raised and healed? Can a man bearing a cup of cold water not bring as timely a gift as any prophet? I think so.

Oh yes, I suppose My angels could supernaturally transport you from place to place all the time, but be honest! Would you not begin to miss using those marvelous miracles called "legs" after awhile? "Holy Ghost" does *not* mean *hocus pocus*. Believe Me, I know Him better than anyone else.

So will you please stop worrying about having a ministry of miracles? Walk on with Me, keep walking in love, and give what you have to give. Miracles will happen, never fear. In fact, you will find them happening all the time!

Helpfully,
Dad

*FROM MY POINT OF VIEW*
I Cor. 2:1-10

Restless Truth Seeker,

The reason I sometimes refuse to inform you is so that I may direct you. Very often information can be a greater hindrance to ministering in the power of My Spirit than you realize. I mean, if at this stage I were to tell you more, you would tend to organize your life in such a way so as to bypass the creative ability of My anointing.

My truth is a living and active *substance*! It just cannot be reduced to mere words, formulas or formats. That is why it has the power to liberate! Do you not remember? The letter kills, but My Spirit gives life; My Spirit and My anointing are one and the same. In fact, My anointing is the very substance and essence of life itself! This being true, your words will have power only as they become the vehicles or the channels of My anointing, My quickening.

And herein lies the problem. Given too much advance notice, some of My more "active" communicators tend to elaborate upon words, plans and concepts so the reality is often lost in the midst of its belabored description. The shadow then supplants the substance and prophecy dwindles to mere poetry. Reality recedes into rhetoric and truth disintegrates into theory, leaving hurting, empty people.

Now do you understand? Too much smoothness smothers and stifles, child. A stumbling sincerity and spontaneity are actually two of My favorite vehicles; but surely you've noticed by now? Keep up the good work! You are doing better than you think — at least from My point of view...

Proudly,
Dad

*HIS FAITH*
Rom. 11:29; Gal. 3:20; II Tim. 2:3

hosen Liberator,

Despite your doubts, I AM at work. As I told you before, I AM preparing a place for you, and very soon you will know beyond all doubt *who* you really are and *why* you were destined to be. Why are you troubled at heart? My callings can never be cancelled, so be at peace about your qualifications, child. I AM. Your gift *will* make room for itself and your own self as well; you will see! In fact, you will soon be seeing *all* things with new eyes from your new position of power and authority. Although you doubt and question, I AM yet committed to honor the deeper faith of your heart — the faith of *My Son* within you.

You apparently forgot, but it is His faith you are living by, is it not?

Proudly Promoting You, I AM!
Father

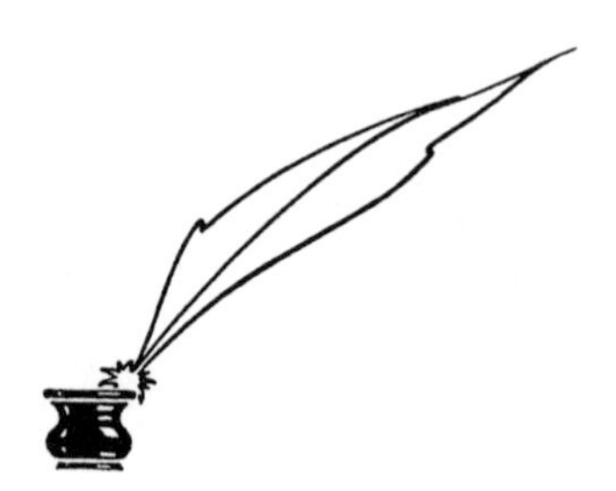

## *REFUSE TO RETREAT*

Rom. 8:17,18; I Cor. 4:1-5

Delightful Deliverer,

When your authority or your validity are questioned, rejoice! Refuse to retreat — even for a moment.

Can you not see that the whole strategy behind the enemy's challenge is to convince you to question your commission and to retreat? Child, "retreat" and "defeat" are alien to heavenly policy! They are words foreign to Kingdom language.

Have you forgotten? Great conquests are often followed by great challenges. Was this not the case even in the ministry of Jesus? Indeed it was. His deeds and His words were often followed by the question, "By what authority does He do these things?" Yes, I knew you would recognize the familiar ring of those words... Be encouraged! Just think of it all as being a "part of the package." I do.

Gladly!
Father

P.S. If you think about it, the *lack* of flak should be the occasion for questions. Don't you agree?

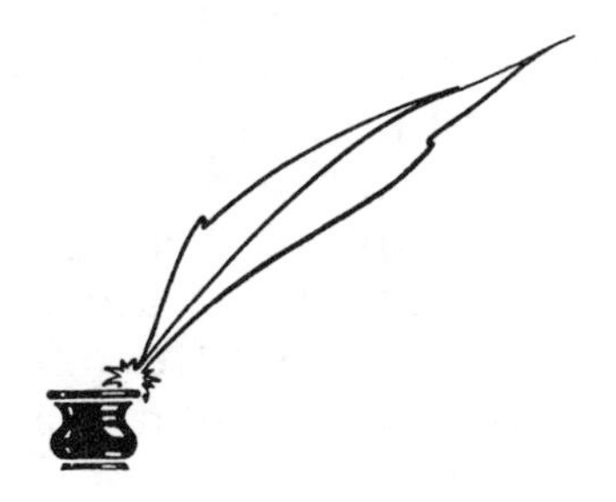

*SOUND JUDGMENT*
Matt. 7:11; John 14:7

Frantic Child,

These days you often hear that I AM a God of judgment, and it is true. I AM. Yet how could I be a God of sound judgment and always be sneaking about *looking* for reasons to reject the children of My own house? Would a sensible earthly father conduct himself in such a manner? You decide.

If you spent more time *with* Me and less with those who merely enjoy *talking* about Me, I know you would be far happier. Has it come to your mind that *all* of Us might be happier if you were? Child, your fear of failure does tend to put everyone else on edge too, so the time has come to lay those fears to rest, once and for all. Come, let Us reason together!

How can anyone who knows anything about Jesus (Who perfectly reflected My nature) portray Me as spiteful and ill-tempered? That fault-finding god of the religionists may be many things, but he could never be Me. Can you imagine such a neurotic, pompous deity dying for his creatures? Hardly. A god so devoid of common decency and good sense could neither love nor give, and he certainly would lack the intelligence to create anything.

Child, that little god could not so much as create a molecule, let alone sustain a universe! No, he could only be what he is — a pitiful projection of fear and guilt, a phantom haunting the hearts of men who think they must scramble to save themselves by earning My acceptance. Such ones have yet to see that "salvation by grace through faith" literally means "trusting Me to free them by love, not merit." My heart aches for them, for they have yet to know Me as I truly am.

Will you be at peace about My judgment? You have gone wrong by listening to the adamant railings of pious but joyless people that I AM allowing to come to the end of themselves. Until the self-righteous reach that place, they can never find Me.

And when you hear the phrase "the fear of the Lord," bear in mind that there is more than one kind of fear. The true fear of the Lord has nothing to do with terror, while much of this "fear of the Lord" noise being blabbed about these days is only religious frenzy. Remember: perfect love casts out that kind of fear. In My way of thinking, "the fear of the Lord" is simply another way of saying, "the wonder and gracious respect for the Lord." Do you suppose there ever could be a better way to think?

Yet the legalists are right about one thing; there really is a great lack of "the fear of the Lord" among My children. But surely the reason is obvious. How can a man feel gracious respect, far less any sense of wonder, toward a Person he hardly knows?

By the way, I really have been missing you lately...

Love,
Dad

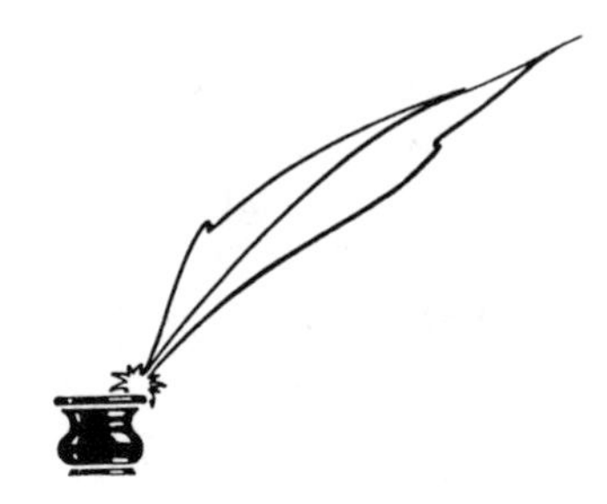

### *ENACT MY TACTICS*

Josh. 6; Prov. 8:6-8; Phil. 1:6

Struggling Son,

Why do you still doubt? Have I not shown you My power by mighty wonders even recently? Of course this battle will not go on forever — certainly not for a lifetime! Do you really imagine that I would lead Us to wage an unwinnable war? Have you ever known Me to give orders for their own sake? Or merely to please Myself? Don't you think if there existed any more qualified to take command I would let them?

You need to remember that My throne is founded on love and wisdom, not brute force. I say a thing is right, not to *make* it right; I say a thing is right because it *is* right. Child, to obey My orders is not to grovel in subservience. It is to discover reality and to learn to rule with Me in My Kingdom! When you follow My commands, you actually enact My tactics. You align with My design and thus find the path to freedom and peace.

If you recall, I once gave some very strange orders to Joshua and the fledgling Israeli nation. Who would ever have guessed that Jericho's walls would crumble at the sound of marching feet, trumpet blasts, and shouting voices? But they did, just the same. Knowing this, why do you grumble about "arbitrary mandates" from your Captain? Have I not always had a unique way of doing things? Carry on! We are too close to victory for quibbling questions now! Besides, in the joy of Our triumph you'll not remember them anyway.

Firmly,<br>Dad

CARRY ON!
...enact my tactics.
ATTACK JERICHO

*WHAT IS TRUTH?*
Heb. 12:7-28

Beloved Adventurer!

What is truth? Truth is timeless, everlasting fact. Truth is the word We use to describe the way reality is, was, and forever is bound to be. Two plus two equals four, blue mixed with yellow is green, and water will forever consist of two parts hydrogen and one part oxygen. There never was a time or a place where two plus two equaled nine, or blue and yellow made purple, or water was oil.

No, truth transcends the trends of men in the same way a real person transcends a cartoon caricature. Truth just is! And why? Because *I AM!* Solid — irreversible — universal Fact; *I AM* what *I AM* — and not even I can change that fact. There never was a time when I was called into existence, and neither is it possible that I should ever cease to exist. I cannot deny Myself, for I AM the Solid Rock. And you should be glad, questioning one.

When I tell you one path leads to life and another leads to death, do you not realize I AM merely showing you how reality happens to work? Child, I show you because I love you. I love you enough to care. Not only do I love you with My affections, I also love you with My ambitions, My aspirations. You might say I have a "champagne taste" where your interests are concerned. I do want the very best for you and, I will admit, My dreams for you are far higher than your young mind can even faintly grasp at the moment.

Honestly!
Dad

*ADVENTURE, NOT ADVERSITY*
Ps. 37:5,6

on, Daughter,

Why not trust My ability to teach you even as I guide your steps? My Anointing rests upon you and you need nothing else. Just commit your comings and goings to Me as you always have! The truths I AM teaching you now exceed the limits of words; otherwise I would have spoken them to you.

Yes, you are right. Lately I have been leading you into realms which, by their very nature, exclude the feasibility of receiving the counsel of men. *Terribly* wonderful of Me, is it not? I do know what I AM doing, children, though you have thought yourselves unprepared for the recent changes. And I will say some of your guesses as to their meaning have been interesting...

Children, children! This is adventure — not adversity! Will you spoil it by complaining? Stop arguing and questioning! Rejoice! If you were unqualified I would not have brought you to this place. As I told you, little ones, I *know* what I AM doing — exactly.

Delightedly!
Dad

## *THE GOD OF RADICAL CHANGE*

Gen. 20

ruth Seeker,

Again, as I have said, nothing shall be impossible to him who believes! I AM making a way — a broad and level way in this present desert. Be assured, I AM. I AM flooding the dry and empty places with rivers of living water, and I AM working the transformation you have long desired to see. How could I not? *I AM the God of radical change!*

But will you cooperate with Me in the process? Will you continue to speak My words and follow the example of your father, Abraham? As We both know, he was far from perfect, yet he did see the son of My promise brought to birth in a miraculous time and in a miraculous way. Yes, Isaac came kicking and squalling into this world despite the failures of his father. And why? Abraham practiced repentance and faith — all the time.

When I called him from the land of his birth, he arose and left all that was familiar, altering his whole life-style to follow My call. He made his home in the land of My promise, though it meant living there as a stranger, an alien, and a nomad dwelling in tents for a season. What a stubborn man he was! He took Me at My word, *acting* like a founding father long before he ever was one. Lovable, indomitable Abraham... Is it any wonder I AM not ashamed to be called his Father?

You see, that man *willed* to act upon My word even in those initial stages when his promised land seemed to promise nothing but a lunar landscape laughing at his dreams. Yet all who would know Me as the God of transformation — in principle — must reenact the acts of Abraham. Child, are you willing? The present desolation is but the preparation for your transformation; truly it is. You have chosen *My* land, and you will not be disappointed, I promise!

Father

*SANDPAPER*
I Cor. 12:14-20

Questioning Son,

I know your friend has his irksome qualities, but he does have many strengths you lack. I have brought you together to complete, not compete. Even those alternating feelings of irritation and compassion I have allowed for your strengthening, believe it or not. I will say it is wrong for you to keep second-guessing his motives and responses. Your brother is not as easy to read as you think but, warts and all, he *is* Mine (just as you are). He is, in fact, rather complex as mortals go, and even I find him complicated — in a delightful sort of way. But then again, you are not as simple as you imagine. So why not leave all the judging to Me? Let Me deal with him; do you mind?

My son does need your influence as much as you need his, but stop *trying* to influence him and relax. Just be joyful, considerate and honest and, of course, be yourself. Also avoid all introspection not instigated by Me. And please! Stop apologizing for your every move. Why speak of "problems" no one else would ever call problems unless you brought them to mind?

Relax! As I have already whispered to your heart, you both are being polished. Yes, you both are serving as sandpaper each for the other (O glorious truth!) and, I humbly concede, the credit belongs to Me.

Count it all Joy!
Father

## *REASONABLE SERVICE*
I Cor. 7:7

ealous Deliverer,

You cannot insist that others walk your walk or live out your calling. Do you not remember how long you were in reaching this place? I do. Understand, little one, I AM not complaining about it, not in the least. No, every faltering step and every hesitation was worthwhile in view of your present development. But that is the point I AM making...

What now appears to you as mere reasonable service once loomed before your eyes as an impassable gulf, and many truths you would never think to question these days you once thought utter nonsense. HA! How well I remember!

Be patient, child. Just keep practicing what you know. Truth is its own advertisement — you know it is. Besides, your ability to succeed in your walk has nothing to do with other mortals walking it with you. You are not alone. I AM with you. Meanwhile, give your friends time to learn and room to grow as I have done for you. Not all learn the same lessons at the same time; but all do learn thoroughly. I see to that. After all, where do you think you got those stubborn tendencies of yours?

Dad

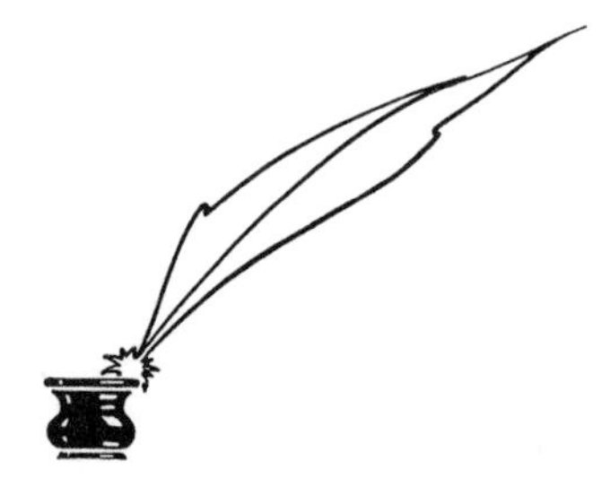

*POINT "B"*
Heb. 11:8-10

Bewildered Deliverer,

What is this "emptiness" you are feeling? I will tell you. You are in transition. In the midst of change there is no choice but to move. In the process of movement, settling in is out of the question. So of course you feel rootless! A tree being transplanted cannot be rooted until it is planted again in good soil.

Ponder this truth and remember it — there is no way to enjoy the comforts of a home and move at the same time. And it is impossible to harvest fruit from a vineyard yet to be.

I know it has seemed like a long journey, but it will be shorter if you will keep this in mind: you aren't supposed to feel satisfied where you are. This isn't home. This is travel.

Meantime, why not enjoy the scenery? You will never pass this way again and one day you will cherish the memories of this trip, if you will take note of them now. Otherwise, you might arrive at point "B" with no stories to tell!

Helpfully,
Dad

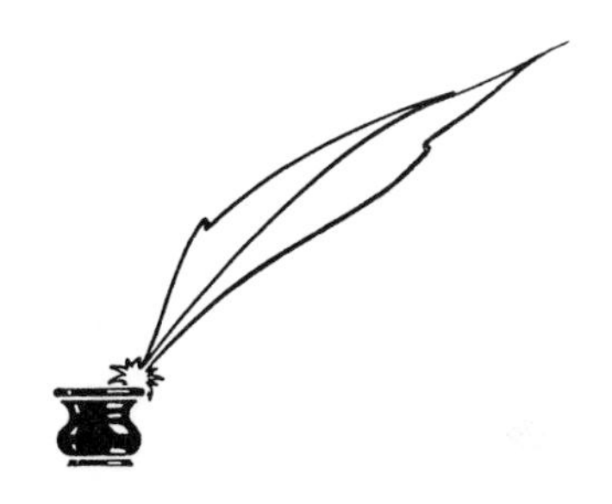

## *THE MEMORIES OF YOUR OFFERINGS*

II Cor. 9:10,11; Heb. 11:1

My Son,

Again you have delighted My heart by your willingness to give. Forsake all fears of having given unwisely and commit the memories of your offerings to Me. No longer look back. Forsake questioning. I AM the One who has led you to give all you have given and I will bless your offerings. I will multiply all back to you again — soon. Very soon, in fact.

Meanwhile, avoid the pitfalls of haste and presumption and abide in My peace. Be steadfast. Decide to abide. Refuse all rationalization or any thought luring you into the frenzy of frantic grasping and self-reliance. Any action taken with even a hint of impatience or fear can never be an act of faith, son. Faith is a solid knowledge of the heart, not a groping, grasping guess of the mind. Faith is far more than believing. Faith is knowing. It is a knowing arising from an inner reality seeded into your spirit by My Spirit. Yes, faith — true faith — is the unshakable conviction that those things you have desired have already been provided. And believe Me, son — they have!

Gladly,
Dad

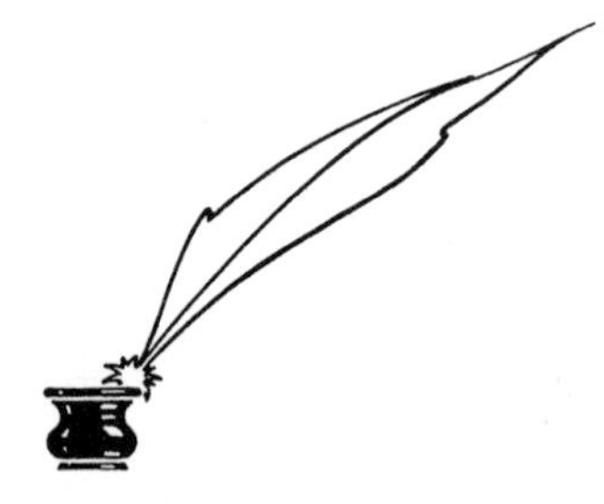

## *THE PASSAGE TO MY GLORY*

Ps. 103:14; Isa. 53

Lonely Liberator,

I know. Your grief has been a silent one, shared only by Me, but I will remind you again — in the solitude of secret sorrows, saviors are formed. Small comfort though it may now seem to be, will you walk on with Me in the knowledge of this? I have borne your griefs, carried your sorrows and fully understood your stumblings. And I have not left you. No, not for a moment. And I AM with you now, holding you. I know how much you yearn to please Me, and the very strength of your desire touches My heart, as much as any gift you ever could give Me.

Knowing this, will you choose to cease all strivings and forsake all fears? Yes, child. Reign with Me! Receive My forgiveness and reign from your position of peace! Offer the sacrifice of praise! Would you know again the power of My Presence? The healing power of My Presence? Then praise, child! Enter into praise, for praise is the passage to My glory and yours! All guilt and all grief will vanish in the light of Our joy. Then you will question nothing except the questions themselves — if you question at all.

Truly,
Dad

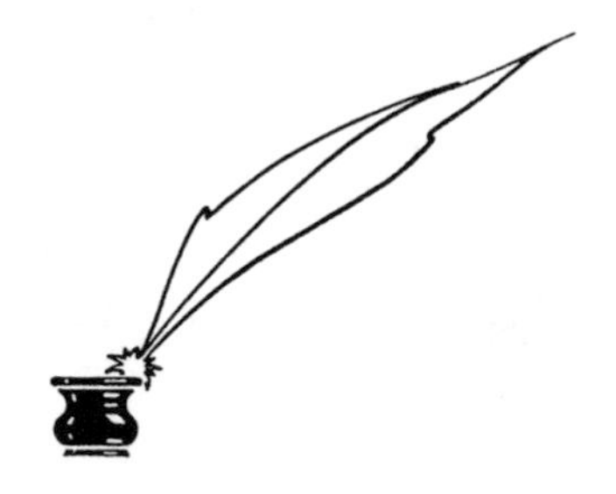

*HAVE A LITTLE TRUST*
Matt. 7:7-11

Fearful Son,

If the son of an earthly father were to ask for bread, would he be given a stone? If he should ask for a fish, would he be given a serpent? You know the answer, so why do you allow those wicked caricatures of God portrayed by ignorant men to frighten you? Son, I appeal to your sense of common decency! Make a list of the qualities one would normally expect to find in a good earthly father! Contemplate fatherhood as it might be without human limitations or corruption, and you will begin to catch a glimpse of the real truth.

Do you honestly think I have some secret motive to disown you? To exploit you? To harass or humiliate you? Am I One to make promises and yet complicate them with hard conditions, rendering them irrelevant and void of fulfillment? Think, son! *Think!* For heaven's sake, have a little trust, will you?

Imploringly,
Dad

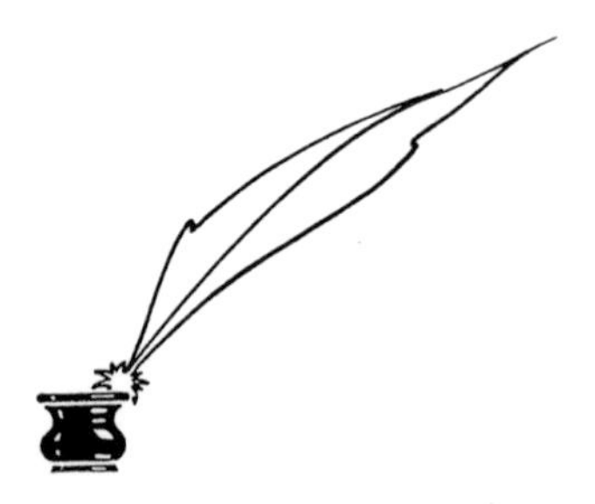

*GOALS*
Rom. 4:3-5

Worried Worker,

Now that you are rigorously applying all of the rules, are you happy? Your treadmill existence seems a great bore to Me, but if it really satisfies you, I will not interfere — although I must admit, the goals you seek are quite different from Mine.

I know you find it hard to believe, but I often simply wish to converse and enjoy Our friendship. I also have delightful gifts to share, but you are too busy...

Child, I only hope you are not doing all of that on My account — I certainly would never ask for it. Dead works are not My department. They are far too costly for you. If you ever get tired, will you please let Me know..?

Tenderly Concerned,
Dad

## *I AM IN CONTROL*

Eph. 1; Eph. 4:7-10; Phil. 1:6

Wounded Soldier,

No, it is *not* your fault. I AM in control. Therefore, commit all "whys" and "wherefores" to Me. Unless you had finally reached the despair of achieving success by your own strength, how would you have come to learn My secrets? How else could you have learned that stubborn dependence upon Me which is so obviously the key to the release of My power? You need to keep in mind that Kingdom policy has always demanded that every upward flight first take on the appearance of a downward plunge. This the world has never understood.

I know. Conflicts have come and contradictions have come as well, but they have come *to pass*. They are but the labor pains preceding the birth of your new vision — *Our* new vision. What? Are you really worried about your reputation? Child, I AM not worried about Mine, so why should either of Us be worried about yours? After all, your reputation is in very good hands — Mine.

Dad

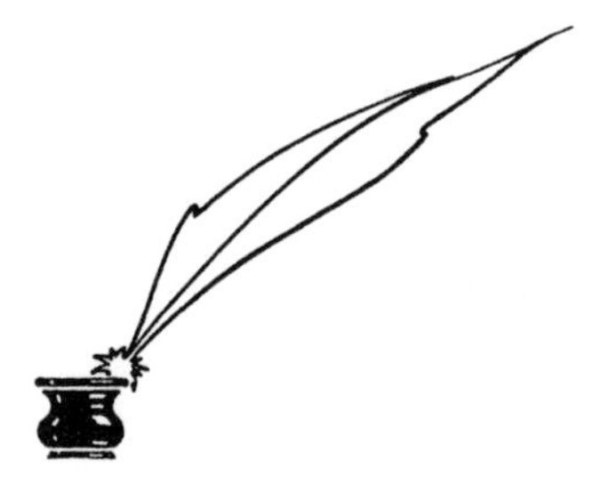

*PROMISES IN PROCESS*
Ps. 105; Heb. 5:14; Heb. 10:35-39

Little Daughter,

Why do you question? Why now? If the promises I whispered to your heart were, as you have feared, merely the wishful thoughts of your mind, then why the fruit? Do you not see that even today you are in the midst of the fulfillment of My words? Rejoice! All promises are, at this very moment, in process. If you cannot believe My words, then will you believe Me for My works?

Review what I have already done! Allow Me to finish, child. Discipline your mind to patience. Practice patience and be at peace. Think on other things. Be thankful. Enjoy!

Your Dad

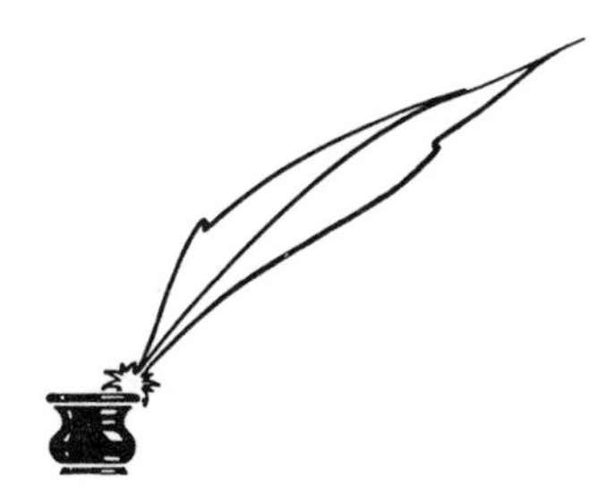

*FACE TO FACE*
Ps. 37:23,24; John 14:27

on,

You *must* become quiet and allow Me to lead you as I always have. I will not disappoint you; you will see. Now, will you turn your thoughts to Me and refuse to strive? You need not try to become anything, because what you already are is exactly what is needed where I AM leading you this day. Besides, if you will receive My peace and simply enjoy being yourself, you will put the others at ease, and they will actually be seeing Me, and not you at all.

Be confident! Choose to assume My quiet and unruffled calm in every motion, transaction and communication. Have I not said, "My peace I give to you; My peace I leave with you"? So there you have it — peace is a gift I have already given you. Receive it. Draw strength from it. Walk in it. Be done with the stress of striving to impress.

Son, if you walk in stress, your friends see Me less and the cycle of fear will continue. As you walk in My peace, My light will increase and My glory will cover and hide you. Then, those you have feared meeting face to face will not be able to see yours for seeing Mine.

Father

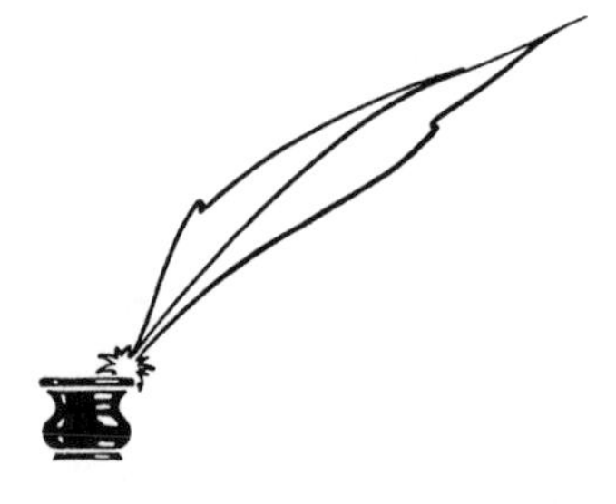

*PURE PLEASURE*
Ps. 37:4; Rev. 4:11

Somber One,

Whether a thing is pleasurable or not has nothing to do with its being right or wrong! Actually, though some will never believe it, My will is found in the fun and enjoyable things more often than not. Are you surprised? Come now! Who ever drummed up the silly notion I was against pleasure? Nonsense. Who do you think began the dance of the constellations? Were not the worlds sung into being amidst angelic shouts of joy?

Of course, We both know many things do offer certain short-lived kinds of joy, but such joys are deceptive and cruel, for they promise happiness while they actually produce death. These — but only these — are the pleasures I would withhold from you, little one.

Now shall I tell you the way to real pleasure? I call it the way of surrender. It is a straight and narrow path, but it does lead to pleasure. Hearty, robust, *pure* pleasure.

Is this not what you seek? Then surrender your desires, each one of them, to Me! Yes, child. Yield every desire to My Spirit, and you will find you are filled with a joy eclipsing all else.

Then having surrendered to My Spirit, do as you wish! And you may as well be prepared — many surprises await you. The way I see it, your problem has been the lack of pleasure; real pleasure, that is...

So you think I AM stodgy, somber, old-fashioned? HA! Follow Me, and you will see... I remain,

Everlastingly Young
and the Ancient of Days,
Your Dad

*BE PATIENT*
Deut. 7:21-23

Little One,

Be patient. I will bring to pass all I have promised. What now seems to you a needless delay — even a backward move — is actually an important step in the necessary process. Child, the pains of healing are similar to the pains of the earlier difficulty, but with one significant difference: they are the result of the steady flow of My Life which is, even now, reversing the damages you have asked Me to mend.

Keep your eyes on Me, for I know an important principle you have forgotten. Often what is quickly acquired is also quickly lost. Therefore, rest! I AM laying a solid foundation which *cannot* be moved.

Faithfully,
Dad

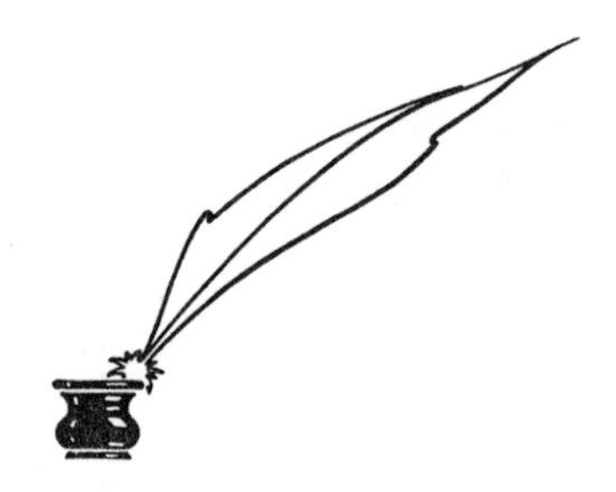

*TOUGH TRAINING*
Book of Job; Ps. 31:22

Diligent Disciple,

Yes, it has been hard, I know, but that tough training period is nearly over now. As I told you before, I have made use of these months to prepare you for promotion — not to punish you. I have been trusting you to trust Me. Thank you for trusting! I realize it has not been easy.

I especially want to thank you for listening for My voice when all those other conflicting voices arose. I know how hard it was — especially when all the others thought they were hearing from Me and kept telling you that you were not. But you were, child. Believe Me, you were! Because you *wanted* My will above all else, you walked in My will.

Now do you see the fruit of those days? You have learned to hear My voice above all the clamor and you are stronger — more resilient. Anyone who really knows you can see it. How can I describe My joy? At last! You chose to stand fast. You set your heart to trust Me, even in those times when the enemy told you I had left you and you had missed the way.

And what about your tantrums? I never took them seriously. They certainly never offended Me. As is often the case with My children, the frustration expressed by your lips had nothing to do with the deeper faith of your heart, expressed by your will. When you told Me you were trusting Me and then willed to walk on with Me, I took you at your word. I admit, you did ask your fair share of hard questions. But consider My servant Job. Did he not do the same? My assessment is this: in all your railing and flailing you never sinned, though We both know your patience did wear thin at times. Dangerously thin. But after all, you were being stretched to your very limits, were you not? I think so.

Stop feeling guilty and enjoy your rest. The rest is a part of the training too. New joys, new powers and new conquests await you, but I do want you prepared to enjoy them!

Delightedly,
Dad

## *MINISTRY MEANS SERVANTHOOD*

Phil. 2; I Thess. 2:4

Searching Servant,

Ministry means servanthood. Being a servant means serving without being thanked or recognized. It often entails giving and going unnoticed, being tired and not rested, sorrowful and not comforted. Servanthood by its very nature implies working behind the scenes, and it always demands quiet reliability on the part of the servant.

Ministry does *not* mean business career. Neither does it mean hobby or pastime. The term "ministry" is light-years removed from the concept of theatrical performance or show business. Ministry can function in these fields, of course. And it should. But the heart of ministry is to serve, not to shine.

Little one, I realize you've been shuttled about lately, ignored and taken for granted. You have also wondered if those to whom you have ministered ever stopped to consider your own private life and needs. Does it matter? Why do you worry about *them?* Why do you seek their honor when you have Mine?

Forever with Joy!
Dad

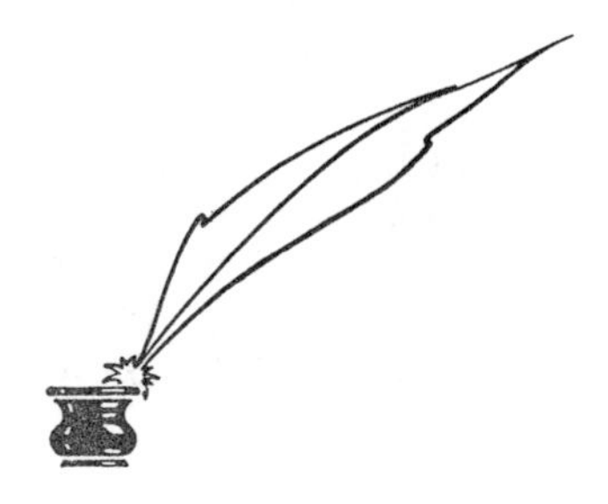

*WAIT ON ME*
Prov. 8:17

Pressured Warrior,

Wait upon Me. I am allowing this time to teach you the power of *living* in My Presence. Have I not promised that if you seek Me with all of your heart you will find Me? The syndrome of seeking Me only in times of adversity must come to an end. You have not understood, little one, but most of the stress compelling you to seek Me for solutions is caused by your lack of constant fellowship with Me.

And yes — I have heard your prayers, and you are right. I have not answered them yet. Why? Child, I have far more to give you than you have asked Me to give. I would not have you settle for less...

Patiently,
Dad

### *REMOVING THE RUBBLE*

Neh. 4:2; I Cor. 3:11-16; Heb. 6:1-3

Fearless Freedom Fighter,

The vision will be fulfilled, but as I told you before, My priority is *you,* not your work. At present I AM rebuilding your walls, but there is rubble which first must be swept away. Now I AM showing you what the rubble is, why it came to be, and how it is to be removed. So be patient with yourself, and be patient with Me.

Some of the rubble is bits and pieces of an earlier "you" which was truly good, but was destroyed when the enemy took advantage of your youth. Never mind. Just let Us get on with the job of clearing it away. You are becoming a new and living temple! I AM making all things new, and the splendor of the new will far surpass the glory of the old. But the sooner the old ruins are removed, the sooner the new "you" will emerge. Therefore, work in joy and work in hope! I AM with you.

And what of those odd-shaped fragments? Surely you recall? Those are scraps from the materials you used when you once set out to rebuild your own walls! Do you remember your rage when I sent the rains to wreck that dreadful little project? I do. We can laugh about it together now, of course. Thankfully, the plan was aborted before it really began to take shape. And now, that will mean less work and time saved for both of Us — provided you resist the urge to analyze every piece and get on with the job of clearing them out...

And do bear in mind that your walls will be altogether unlike your foundations. It would be wrong to expect the same materials and procedures at this point. Walls are not supposed to be made like foundations; they are supposed to be made like *walls.* Remember this. Enjoy the new! Keep working in hope! I AM!

Father

*SANCTITY OR SANCTIMONY?*
Matt. 12:3-8; Matt. 15:1-20; Rom. 2:28,29

Happy Adventurer,

Sanctimony is the preference of procedure to people. True sanctity is the preference of people to procedure. Yes, the Sabbath is for man, not man for the Sabbath, and if you follow this rule you will find your heart to be aligned always with Mine.

The sanctimonious work to be seen of men, but the sanctified work for the healing of men. The religious practice principle for the sake of preeminence. My liberators give their lives for the sake of My people.

Will you let this dispel those phobias of yours about sanctification, son? Personally, I think you could do with more of it...

Honestly, but Cheerfully,
Dad

*A FINE DONKEY*
Num. 22:22-33; I Cor. 4:20; I John 4:17

Daring Deliverer,

Why are you so depressed? Why do you think satan would send his unwitting victims to discourage you unless he were hoping to rob you of your courage?

I never commissioned you to argue, persuade, or answer all questions! You know very well that My wisdom is revealed in power, not in talk. Anyone can talk! Did I not once anoint a fine donkey of Mine to demonstrate this to a very foolish prophet? Obviously, that noble beast had more prophetic insight than did her master — agreed?

Take courage! I called you to demonstrate My power — to *free* men, not to please them. Now go forth and do it! In this world there is no painless way to love; I know. Carry on. Forgive the faultfinders, cast aside your doubts and dare to be what I called you to be! If you choose to dance to the tune of your critics, you will only be playing into the enemy's hands. I have need of you. Will you put on My armor and spring forth to free the captives? Be bold! Release My Word and behold its power to vindicate itself! The changed lives of your hearers will shine with such splendor, all questions will be reduced to rubble!

If you still have any doubt about it, you need to remember that We are in this mission together. Have I ever left you stranded?

Tenderly,
Dad

*SHOWER ENCOURAGEMENT*
Col. 2:2,3

Pressured Child,

Constructive criticism can be very draining to a man already exhausted and spent, so instead of sharing your helpful insights today, why not shower encouragement? Pure encouragement. Undiluted with tactful reservations or timely hints. Yes, look for the praiseworthy things and celebrate them! Applaud them! Praise your loved ones and fellow workers! The strength they will draw from your praise will cause them to excel far beyond the levels of performance any critical analysis might bring.

Start making this a habit, will you, child? I AM trusting you. I have need of you...

Entreatingly,
Dad

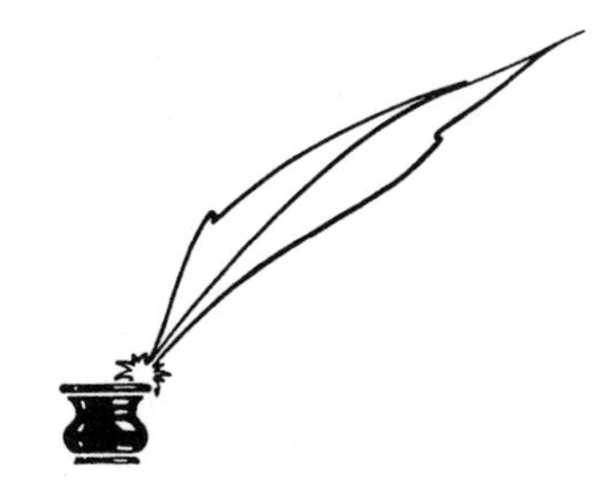

### *BUFFETING*

Matt. 25:14-30; II Cor. 12:7-10

Bold Pioneer,

I know you find it perplexing, but the whole issue of guidance comes back to trusting in Me, not outward appearances.

Before I address your question as to *how* you seem to err at times — speaking words not Mine and taking faulty steps despite all precautions — I should remind you: I AM happier, far happier, with the man who attempts what he honestly thinks I AM leading him to do than with those who do nothing for fear of mistakes. My policy is to work all things together for good for all who love Me enough to walk in My purpose and call. This you know by experience.

Now. In answer to your question, you need to remember there are times when satan seems to gain a momentary advantage in the battle. He harassed the Son of Man, he hindered the apostle Paul, and he will do the same with you.

Also, there is another factor at work you should consider. I call it *buffeting*. Actually, it is more than a factor — it is a principle. And believe Me, all who walk in revelation knowledge *will* stumble across it, sooner or later. Paul certainly could tell you about it. When that principle crops up, you will blunder into obstacles, collide with opposition, and wade through sheer trivia. In those times of buffeting, you will find yourself constantly praying, while constantly wondering if your prayers are even being heard. Moreover, you will take steps and speak words in your ministry that are mysterious, to say the least. And when you do, there will always be critics who will delight in questioning your validity.

Why do I allow this? Child, too much easy success would make you unbearable — honestly. So I use those little "flaws" of yours to cause you to pause to seek Me. Because they drive you into My arms, they become My opportunity, and *your salvation*. Meantime, your ineptness also beams a ray of hope to others who need assurance that I AM pleased to work in the weakest of vessels. I do love earthen vessels, you know.

And remember, what may now appear to be a false move or a spurious revelation will make sense in retrospect — at least, most of the time. But whatever happens, will you continue to trust Me? Jesus was condemned as a false prophet when He foretold the ruin of the temple, and He was the Prophet of all prophets, the very Prototype of all prophets. Yet He witnessed the vindication of His words *decades later* — from eternity. If you are serious about doing His work, is it asking too much that you be willing to take His risks?

Trustingly,
Father

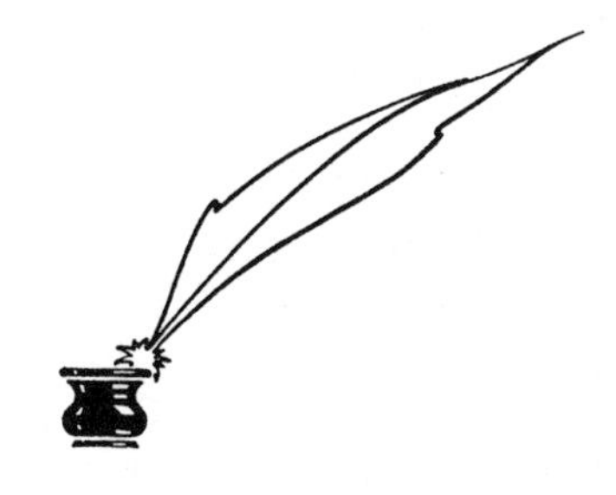

## *I BELIEVE IN YOU*

John 16:12,33

Chosen Deliverer,

I AM the One who called you, so will you believe Me when I tell you? Son, *I* believe in you and that is all that matters. Too late? How little you know Me, young one... It is never too late if you are walking with Me, for all times are Mine — including yours.

Trust Me! Even if you had missed the mark ten thousand times ten thousand, I yet make all things new. Your every stumbling and setback will be used to the fullest in My economy, you will see! You are destined to be a compassionate deliverer and you will have healing gifts to share. As you share them, you will spare many the heartaches you have known.

Already I AM multiplying the good you did accomplish in your desert years — those days when you walked in your own ways. Yes, it is now My joy to reckon all as done unto Me, so I AM accrediting your every act of love to the record of your faithful ministry.

Now will you accept My gifts and please stop mouthing all that nonsense about fairness? Can I not determine just wages for My workers? We will speak of it no more. Enough! Let Us dry those tears. You will need clear vision to enter the new door I AM now opening.

And lest you fret about having too little time left, perhaps I should remind you — I have been known to do remarkable things with very small quantities. Do you remember the miracle of the five loaves and two fishes? Actually, that was one of My smaller miracles...

Son, I have even more to tell you, but you are too young to bear it now. Meanwhile, will you please be at peace about time? I AM the King of *all* Ages. I AM the Master of *all* times — including yours. Time without end — I AM!

Yours Forever,
Dad

*I WANT YOU TO SEE*
Gal. 5:22-24; Col. 1:9-14

Son,

Self-control is indeed a fruit of the Spirit. It is a by-product of Spirit-inspired vision. Self-control derives its strength from the joy of having purpose.

When a man sees purpose — when his spirit is inflamed with a vision of his royal destiny — anything, good or bad, which would distract him from achieving his goals lacks power to attract him.

Self-control is not will power. Have you noticed? Self-control is a result. It springs from the power naturally released by purpose itself. I want you to see your purpose. I want to ignite your spirit with a vision of your mission — daily. When you start seeing what you are *and* what you are about, you will easily avoid those things you can do without.

Self-control is meaningless without mission. It is not even possible, and even if it were, it would be nothing but a mockery — a vanity above all vanities. But I think We both agree on this point...

Seek Me early. I will teach you to order your days. Remember, your victory is contained in the vision. It is yours for the asking.

Always,
Dad

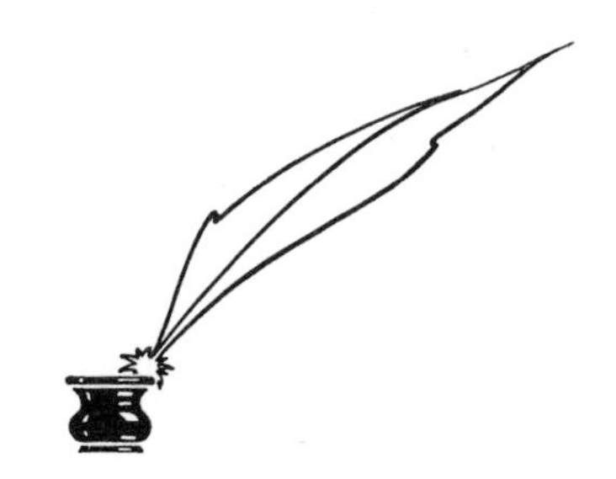

*OBSTACLE COURSE*
I Sam. 17:32-37

Frustrated Fighter,

Why have I been leading you through this obstacle course of pressured events? Why the unreasonable demands, the dangers? I have allowed them for one practical reason: to deliver you from fear once and for all.

I have known what you had yet to discover, child. Every exposure to the unexpected, the unreasonable and the undeserved has been an inoculation of sorts. Oh yes, I do have all kinds of strategies — have you noticed? Yet have you noticed this? More and more you are coming to trust Me; less and less you are fearing the future. You see, every time those threats have reared their silly heads, I have repeatedly shown you My power to bring them to naught. And I have been building an inner peace in you at the same time.

Do you realize how much more pleasant your company has become for All of Us lately? Ah yes, the new you is far easier to enjoy — I assure you. Not that We ever loved you any less, of course. We're all simply glad the real you has finally arrived. But, no doubt, you are the most glad of all!

Proudly, Joyfully,
Dad

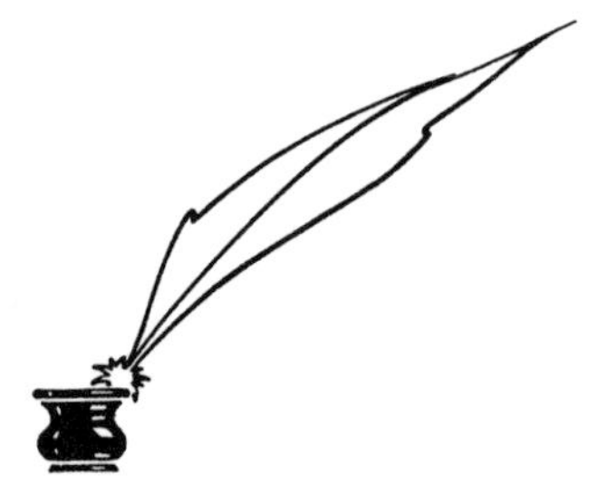

*COLORED LIGHTS*
Isa. 55:2; Eph. 2:1-10

Fervent Servant,

I AM glad for your servant's heart, truly I AM, but may I remind you again? Any action taken apart from Me is a departure from Life, and every step away from Me is a step into unreality — no matter how noble or praiseworthy it may appear to be of itself. The fact remains, to leave Me is to leave life and reality and to enter the realm of the living dead. Though its entry be lit with heraldically colored lights flashing the promise of freedom, beyond flickers a dim fantasy world teeming with smiling faces masking broken hearts.

Tragically, many of My children dwell there most of the time. It is true. Though the housing fees are astronomical and the service shoddy, do you realize most refuse to move for fear of displeasing *Me*? It has just never occurred to them that stirring up more religious activity was the last thing I had in mind when I sent Jesus to your world.

Shall I tell you why He came? He came to adopt children for Our Royal Family! Our plan was to nurture them, crown them with life, and enthrone them with Us as co-regents in the Kingdom of Light. Heaven knows We were not recruiting servants. Beloved children with servants' hearts, yes, but servants, no. We had quite enough as it was. Good ones, too!

So do you mind My asking a few personal questions? Why do you weary yourself rushing about looking for things to do, leaving Me behind to watch? Is it really Kingdom business you are doing? Or are you trying to earn My love? But child! How can you earn what you already have? Are you seeking to earn the love of mere men? If their love can be bought, it is false. Why do you toil for that which is not Bread and settle for worthless wages?

Will you return to Our Kingdom courts? My heart aches for your pain...

Brokenly,
Father

*FRET NOT*
Ps. 37; I Thess. 5:18

Dedicated Disciple,

Do you realize the command to "fret not" carries equal weight with any other command of Mine? Think about it.

What do you suppose would become of the more obvious sins of covetousness, revenge, lust and infidelity if worry were forever banished? The foundation of all sin is fear, and worry is but another form of fear — agreed?

So worry is always wrong. Yes, even if it comes to worrying *about* worrying — or even worrying about *not* worrying — worry itself is still lethal to the heart. In everything give thanks, child! And your thanks will establish what the mind thinks. Always.

By the way, have you ever paused to ponder how often I think about you? I think you'd be amazed if you knew...

Love,
Dad

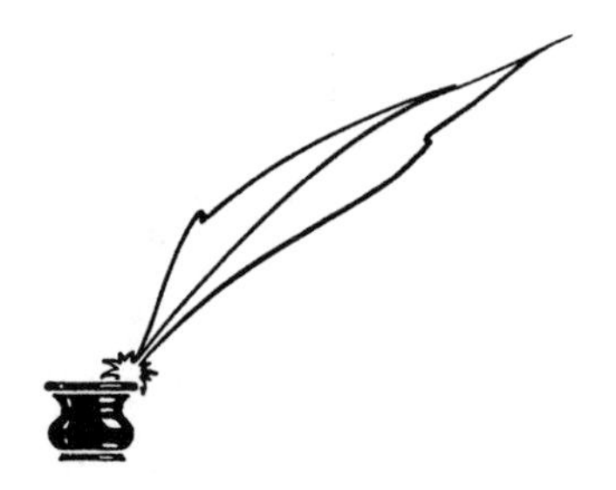

*WASTED TIME*
Rom. 8:28

uestioning One,

Why do you worry about "wasted" time? Child, you have experienced some errors and a few false starts, but never mind... Redeeming time and fresh beginnings are two of My mightiest mercies! If you will follow Me, I will cause every reversal to count as rehearsal for even greater victories than were previously planned.

Child, I make all things new, including you. Will you rest in this assurance? I AM the Master of time, and there is no loss in Me.

Truly!
Father

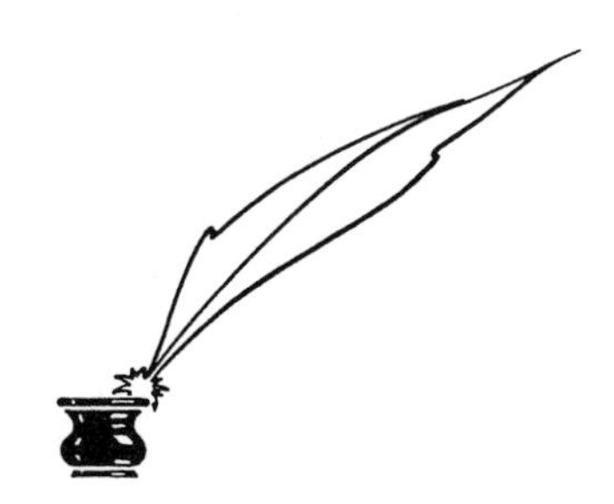

*TWO-FOLD PROCESS*
Ps. 66:16-20; Heb. 10:35,36

Sorrowful One,

If you were *trying* to live two life-styles — if you were justifying sin or seeking to harm another — that would be different. Then I would be forced to let you feel the full impact of your ways. I would laugh at your reasonings, ignore your pretended prayers and weep for your delusion. But such is not the case. I told you this earlier, but I will tell you again; I have seen your tears and heard your cries. I AM holding you now.

Don't give up. I haven't. Your sacrifices of praise and even your outbursts of frustration are all part of a two-fold process. You are experiencing the death throes of the old and the birth pains of the new, and there just is no other way for this deliverance to come forth. Soon you'll not even think to question the process. You'll be too busy enjoying the *substance* born of the process.

Remember, I cannot lie...

Faithfully,
Father

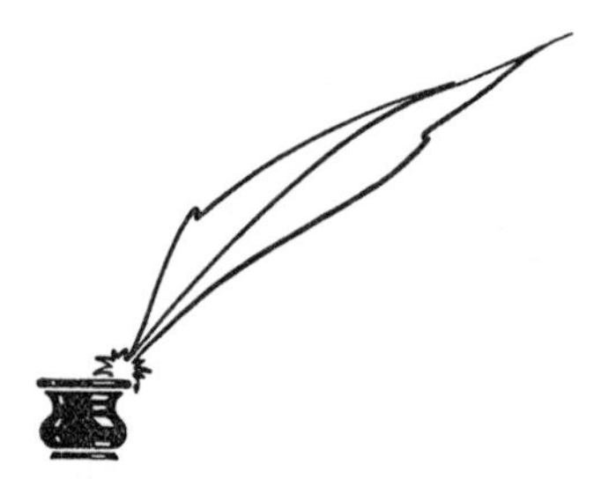

*REMEMBER*
Isa. 52:14; John 3:16

Worried Child,

I AM just, pure and holy. My love is limitless and seeks not its own. When those dark thoughts cloud your mind, causing you to question My love, I ask that you do one thing: remember the cross.

See it now. See the One crucified. See the humiliation, the horror of Innocence disrobed, mutilated and bleeding. Pain racks His every atom. Each gasp of air is agony untold. His every nerve is a conduit of fire.

Can you hear Him cry? No one else can either, but I can. I hear it forever — how could I forget it? It's almost the sound of a boy — a stifled, intermittent cry it is...

No, child, don't turn away. Not yet, please. Do you see the thorns piercing His brow? The disfigurement of His face? The spikes splitting His hands and His feet? The jeering crowds at the foot of His cross? They didn't kill him. They would have if they could have — but they could not. He *gave* His life. He shielded His enemies who were worthy of death by dying Himself in their stead. He suffered murder to save His murderers. He suffered shame to save His mockers. And He would do it again. Again and again. And so would I. Is this not the destiny of Perfect Love in a fallen world?

This is the way love is, and this is the way I AM. Never forget it.

Entreatingly,
Father

*A LONELY PATH*
Obad. 1:21; I John 4:17

Recovering Restorer,

Be at peace. Know you are protected. Yes; you are right. I have allowed a lonely path for you — a path others have assessed from their surface view as an easy one. Never mind. It is Our view that counts, not theirs.

Rejoice! You are specially chosen and hand-picked. I have called you to demonstrate My heart to a hurting generation. The world is weary of words and so am I. Therefore I AM raising up an army of saviors, and as a leader in that army you have been chosen to *demonstrate* My saving character to many silent sufferers. For so long I have yearned, through My family, to love into wholeness the broken and wounded. You will exemplify how it is done.

Be at peace about your lack of knowledge. I have purposely foiled your attempts to become a theologian. I need redeemers, not religionists. And why have I allowed you to work in weakness? To carry a burden which has forced you to fall continually upon My grace? I seek deliverers, not destroyers. Restorers, not rejecters. Your own need of mercy has made you a vessel of mercy — a compassionate counselor and life-giver. You know it is true. I have kept you, formed you, withstood you at times, but always upheld you. And I have counted it all pure joy!

So you thought you would never be free, did you? Now do you see the purpose of those years of searching? Your seeming lack of solutions? These laid the foundation for your freedom today. Keep giving grace and keep loving sinners. I do. And stay committed to the *good* news of My power.

I AM!
Father

your own need of Mercy
has made you a
Vessel of Mercy
. . . to
demonstrate
my character
to many
silent sufferers.
©1989

## *ONE OF THOSE TOMORROWS*

Ps. 37:5,6; II Tim. 1:12

on,

When you are seeking Me and surrendering your steps to My strategies — when you are pursuing truth with all your heart — forget the flak. Stop worrying about your lack and stop hesitating about decisions. Make choices! Let the results be My responsibility, and refuse to judge the fruit of your work until I clearly lead you to do so.

All things are not as they at first appear to be. Start seeing all interruptions and confrontations, shortages and surprises, not as obstacles, but opportunities. These give you cause to pause — to rest — while I resolve. Your resting will release you into revelation otherwise unobtainable.

And remember. Today is one of those tomorrows you asked Me to keep many yesterdays ago. I AM.

Always,
Your Father

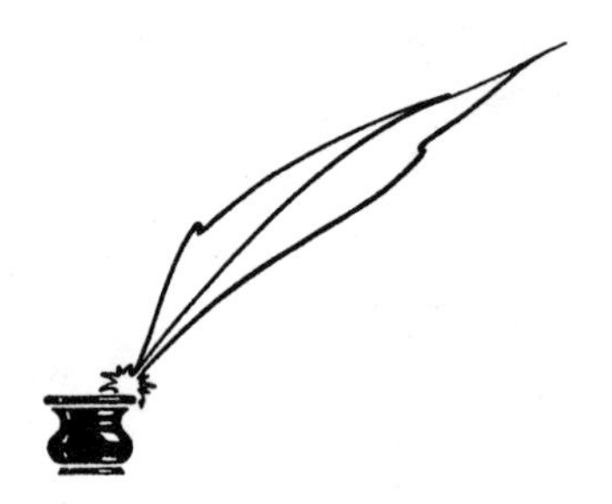

*THE GOSPEL TRUTH*
II Tim. 2:3

Questioning Conqueror,

How many times must I tell you? This is warfare — not a pleasure cruise. True, I did promise that if you asked for a good gift I would not give you a counterfeit. But I certainly never promised easy solutions and quick fixes. I did promise you *Myself* — but you have yet to appreciate the magnitude of that promise.

You do seem to have a problem with waiting, don't you? Has it occurred to you that your impatience may just be the problem? Child, I AM not scolding you and neither am I offended by your questions. But you do need to realize that it *is* a war We are fighting. It is naive to become cynical just because of a few setbacks.

Is a battering ram considered useless simply because it fails to smash the enemy's defenses in a single thrust? Your prayers — those times you spend walking and talking with Me in solitude — are exactly like a battering ram. In fact, Our communication, in itself, is the most powerful weapon We possess. Can you not see why the evil one would try to talk you out of it? Use it!

By the way, if you're waiting to become "worthy," please stop. You already are. Christ has made you worthy. That is the gospel truth. Walk in it.

Love,
Dad

## *LOVE CANNOT FAIL*

I Cor. 13

Worried Warrior,

Always remember. God is Love and Love never fails. Love *cannot* fail. Repeat this truth again and again. Commit it to memory. Let it be forever imprinted upon the tablets of your heart. And never forget. All that is stated about Love in the Bible applies *first* to *Me*.

Love thinks evil of no one. Love is not rude, but kind. Love is not proud, and neither does it keep score of wrongs suffered. Love redeems and never rejects. Further, Love looks for the praiseworthy — always; and it does not seek its own interests.

You must learn to think of Me in this way, for this is the way I AM. Why do you believe the corrupted conceptions? Hasn't your own experience confirmed the truth? Believe in the God who has saved you — many times! If I were looking for reasons to reject you, I could not be Who and What I AM: Love.

Any message of "holiness" engendering hopelessness is of hell, not heaven. Remember this. Any use of scripture that produces despair is warped and sinful. Many can parrot the scriptures, but few have learned the heart of their Author. Who can impart My love? I AM counting on you.

Peace. Your sins are forgiven.

Forever in Love,
Father

## *THE ORIGINAL AMONG ORIGINALS*
John 7:46

Searching Son,

How many times do you suppose Jesus taught about going the second mile, or forgiving one's enemies or seeking first the Kingdom? He repeated Himself *repeatedly* — as any good teacher should. So it is a mistake to adopt the mindset that your every word must fall upon the ears of your hearers as something "new."

I sent Christ to impart life, not to present original-sounding spiritual novelties. His words, His deeds, His attitudes and His very Person were all vehicles through which My life came forth. He expended no efforts *trying* to be "fresh" or "stimulating." But He did spend time with Me.

And what Jesus learned in My fellowship affected Him so profoundly that all He did and said reflected the power of My presence. As a result, though He never tried to be interesting, He was. Your Lord was sometimes accused of having a demon, but no one ever called Him dull. Christ never sought originality, but throughout history His friends and His enemies alike have declared Him to be the Original among originals. He never studied a course in psychology, nor did He seek the advice of the "image consultants" of the day. Yet there never lived a man more powerful, more persuasive or more convincing than Jesus of Nazareth. That is why the authorities had Him crucified. They feared the Nazarene might change the face of history. And He did. All by walking with Me.

Helpfully,
Dad

*THE DESERT*
Matt. 3:15-17; Matt. 4:1-11; Luke 4:13,14

Compassionate Deliverer,

A desert experience almost always follows the anointing. Your Lord was driven into the desert after My Spirit descended upon Him like a dove, and His life is the master plan for all of My deliverers. Yes, Jesus truly is the Way. As the Dove led Him into My purposes and the desert prepared Him for power, so it will be for all of Our Family. That pattern can never change. Those who would be vessels of Mine must be tested, for the passage of My power demands the durability only the tests can build.

Now do you understand the void you so often feel after your mightiest victories? The vulnerability? The sheer terror of falling? The Spirit, by virtue of what He is, floods to the surface your flaws, for your sake. By that He spares you the ruin which would result from the co-habitation of His fire with your flesh. Then, as those weaknesses and sins are renounced, they give way for a greater release of My power.

Will you stand strong in the joy of this truth? Be tempered by the testings that follow the anointing and you will wear the crown of life. Even more, you will wield the authority of that crown and do the powerful works of Jesus — proficiently! I promise.

Father

*LET ME VINDICATE*
Luke 6:27-30

Pressured Peacemaker,

Let Me vindicate you. Allow Me to be the Lord you have confessed Me to be. Stop worrying about your brother's opinion and go on doing what I have called you to do.

You have sought to gain the understanding of one who has much to learn before any of your words can even begin to make sense to his mind. You have tried to win his heart. Well done. You have tried — earnestly tried — and I have seen it and I AM pleased. Now will you leave the results to Me?

Cease all self-castigations, all self-justifications and all your rationalizations *now*. Henceforth I will do the correcting, the defending, the explaining. And you? You will be happy again. And I do think it's time you were...

Truly!
Dad

*STRETCHED*
Jer. 1

uestioning Conqueror,

You do exercise more influence than you realize, and your insights carry more weight than you know. Your low assessment of your value is quite different from the admirable impression you leave with others; so stop listening to lies. Start trusting your gifts and stop trusting those doubts! If the enemy can persuade you to abdicate, not only will he score a victory against you, but he also will rob others. He will deny them the benefits you alone were designed to deliver.

I know. You feel inept, insecure and insignificant. At times you feel as inexperienced as a child. But strange as it seems, I AM healing you of this mindset by promoting you. I AM now placing you in a position which demands more than you *think* you have to give.

Yes, at the moment you are being *stretched.* I want you to realize the prized possession you actually are to My heart! I AM awakening potentials and unveiling gifts within you that you have been too blind to see. I AM purposely giving you some challenging assignments to break the confinements caused by your unbelief. I want to rid you, once and for all, of that mediocre view you have held of yourself.

I understand your frustration. But as a sensible Father, I harbor no illusion that My children will always agree with My policies — at least, not at the outset. Nevertheless, I do expect them to trust the decisions of One Who is older and wiser. Child, are you willing?

You will come to enjoy your new post, but you'll not have time to fret about that imagined inferiority of yours in the meanwhile. No, you'll be too busy, but I think you'll also be much happier. So for now I AM putting you in a strategic position to instruct others. I happen to know there is no better way for one to learn than to have to teach.

Cheer up! Since I have chosen to trust you, does that not give you cause to trust yourself? You are My creation, so isn't it reasonable to think that I must surely know more about you than you do?

Truly,
Dad

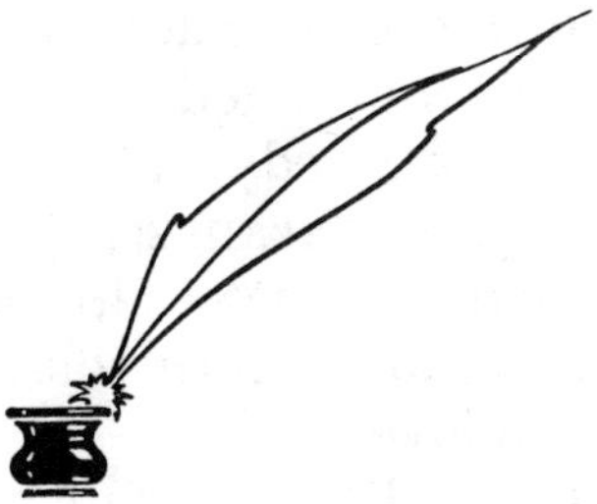

### *HEAVEN AND HELL*

Ps. 112:4; Prov. 1:32,33; Rom. 14:17; Gal. 6:7-10

Restless One,

In answer to your question of how a loving God can allow there to be a hell, consider this: heaven and hell are conditions of the heart before they can ever be anything else, and a man conditions his heart for his final destiny by his own habitual choices. It is choice that constructs character, fashioning it for either everlasting joy or endless torment. Thus, every decision a man makes, whether great or small, to some degree affects his destiny. It is the law of cause and effect — the way reality is bound to work and will always work. Every choice contributes to the design, disposition and final fixation of the inner self. Yes, choice is the chisel by which the character is carved.

Child, I banish no one! And neither do I assign men and women to heaven or hell. All are *designed* for their destinies by their own repeated decisions. There can be no heaven for the soul conditioned for hell. Streets of gold would burn the feet of a greedy and miserly man far more than the flames of outer darkness. But the grateful and generous-hearted will see heaven in the worst of hells. It is written, "Light will arise in the blackest night for the man of integrity and love."

Heaven would be the worst of hells for the soul unprepared for its environment. If a man has repeatedly refused the joys of heaven offered him in earthly life, how could he desire them in the life to come? He would have actually grown to prefer the perverted "joys" of hell. A woman who had learned to enjoy self-pity and complaining would never feel at home in a realm of thanksgiving and praise. A man consumed with ambition could find no pleasure in a land of love and submission. Lust, at any cost, whether for pleasure or power or possessions, eventually erodes everything worth having. When a man's lust becomes his idol, it literally destroys his capacity to make a righteous choice. Such a man would never recognize Me if he saw Me — nor would he ever want Me if he did.

Every day presents fresh opportunities to choose life or death, love or hate, heaven or hell. So now do you see why I keep talking about the importance of thanksgiving, love and forgiveness? If you practice choosing these you will find yourself already in the habit of heaven.

Helpfully,
Dad

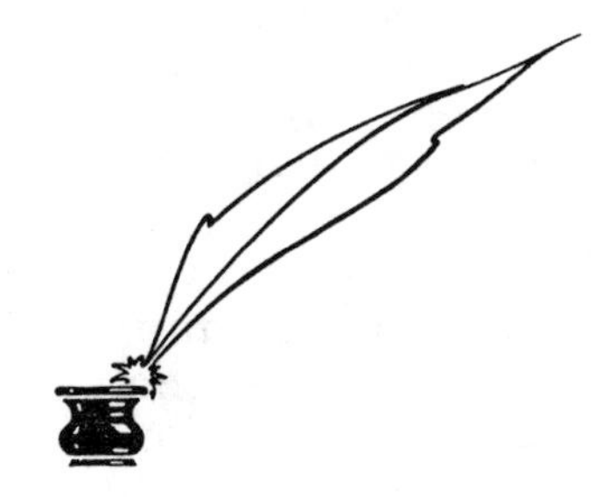

## *THE WAY LOVE IS*

Rom. 11:1-6

Beloved Rebel,

Believe it or not, I too find religion boring — extremely boring. In fact, I often find it annoying. Has it occurred to you that I might be interested in many other subjects? I AM. My range of interest just might be even wider than yours!

I like various sports, arts, writing, music — and jokes. And although some would be shocked to hear it, I enjoy theater and dancing immensely. And why not? I AM the Inventor, if you recall. I also happen to be very fond of animals. Or haven't you noticed? Oh yes; I AM an incurable bird watcher and sparrows are some of My favorites. Geography and astronomy never cease to interest Me, and I also delight in chemistry and micro-biology. No doubt you have observed this.

Yet, like yourself, I AM repelled by meaningless rituals and routines. The realm of organized religion is very dull and drab, I think. Its goals and interests are mostly unrelated to Mine. If I attend a religious event, I do so strictly from a sense of duty — you can be sure of that. I make it a policy to attend only if I AM invited, so, as you can surmise, I rarely go at all. By that I mean My *heart* is not in it. In one sense it would be impossible for Me not to be there. Perhaps that is what might be called one of the less fortunate aspects of being omnipresent?

We have more in common than you think! I find flowery speeches a bore, tradition tedious and I hate religiosity. But I do love people. That is why I can't just simply give up on the Church. But isn't that the way love is? Love doesn't have an "off and on" switch. At least, My kind never has.

Besides, when I think of the Church I think of My family. In My view, the religious rat race is a universe removed from what the Church is really about.

Keep an open mind and an open heart. I AM arranging some new contacts I think you're going to like.

All My Love,
Dad

*WITH NO REGRETS*
I Pet. 2:19-23

Son,

Forgiveness is an act of the will. One must *decide* to forgive and then *choose* to forget. I understand. The memories of the rejections, the betrayals and deceptions do have a way of seeping back to the surface of your mind. But have you ever stopped to think about why? They always return when you withdraw into introspection and neglect to enjoy the gifts I have showered upon you.

Of course, as you have noticed, I do keep sending distractions and interruptions to draw you away from your introspection. I also divert your plans to guard you from those who talk too much about the past. I shield you — continually — but I cannot protect you from *you*. You have asked that I heal your broken heart, but will you cooperate with Me? Stop analyzing yourself and others — please... Allow Me to suture the wound.

I want you to get on with *enjoying* your life! New delights await you and I want you to experience them. But how will you ever see what lies ahead if you keep looking behind? Forgive and forget, son. I do — constantly. But surely you have noticed by now? I do it gladly, with no regrets, all the time.

Tenderly Yours,
Dad

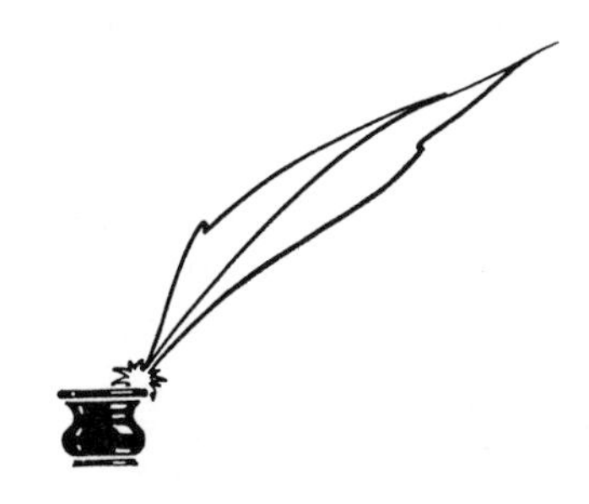

## *WHAT SORT OF VEGETABLE?*

Eph. 4:26-32

Worried Child,

When I said I couldn't protect you from yourself, I didn't mean it in the way you understood it. Of course I protect you from yourself! I do it all the time. I do it by softening the impact of the blows you inflict upon yourself when you act in haste, anger or fear. But I cannot keep you from wielding those blows unless I destroy your power to choose.

Is that what you want? What sort of vegetable do you want to become? A plant with a human shape would be a remarkable curiosity in Our Kingdom. Indeed it would. But the Image of My Son deserves a higher expression. At least, I think it does. Turning conquerors into cabbages is just not My department. That is the work of the enemy.

How does he do it? By deception, of course! He has no other power. When he teaches a man to habitually reject responsibility for his own actions and to see himself as a victim of fate, that man loses his grip on life. And the more entrenched in blame-placing and excuse-making he becomes, the more like a vegetable he becomes.

So don't you think it's time you stopped blaming others for your miseries? Take responsibility! Are you afraid to say "I'm sorry" or "I was wrong"? Don't be. It's not as bad as you think. Have you let the sins of others sour your outlook? Repent. You'll like the way it feels, I promise. Your happiness can be the responsibility of no one but yourself. No slight or wrong committed by anyone can sabotage your joy, unless *you* let it. So forgive and forget. And as you do, also forgive yourself. I already have.

Forever with Love,
Dad

## *SCRUBBY LITTLE UGLIES*
Col. 2:20,21

Remorseful Restorer,

The lapses were foreseen by Me. Looking back, you wonder why they happened at all. Because many of your mistakes appear so meaningless, viewing them from hindsight, you often flush with shame. But may I tell you a secret?

I never wanted you to fail, but because I created you with free will I knew that you sometimes would. Knowing this, I planned and actually programmed each day of your life to be permeated with mercies. Thus, all things — including your failures — *must* work together for your good while you are learning to live by My law of love. Remember, learning is a process. No one learns to walk without stumbling.

Lately you have been discovering how your lapses can become lessons to remind you of your need for My grace. Sustained "success" rooted in the strength of the flesh is superficial and deceptive. It is a glistening bubble only the pin of an *obvious* sin can burst. No, I did not cause it, but I did allow it.

Understand. I want to save you from every sin, of course. But I don't want you just doing "right things." I want you doing right things for right reasons. I want you to be right *inside.* Why are you in such a hurry? I AM not. Frankly, those scrubby little uglies that have surfaced lately *needed* to become visible. You needed to see your inability. You also needed to see My love in action far more than you needed to see any outward show of success. Keep trusting My love for your holiness.

Forever,
Your Dad

*THE CLASSROOM*
I Pet. 1:3-9

hild,

You are exactly where you need to be right now. Believe Me. If all external factors instantly changed, the lessons you are learning now would still be the same. The classroom could be a hotter one or a colder one, but it could not be a better one than this present one. There are many possible environments in which you could learn the truths I AM teaching you today. If you flee the present one, you will find another one, but I must warn you: it will be a harder one.

You asked Me to guide your steps, keep your tomorrows and turn your blunders into blessings. Do you remember? Well, I have. I AM doing it right now, in fact.

Father

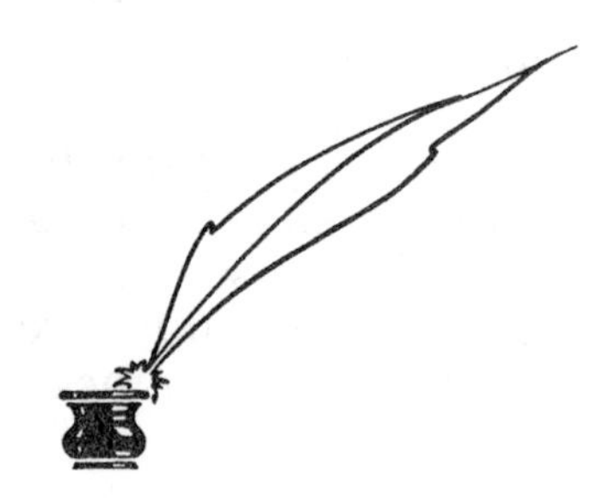

*TOUGH FAITH*
Rom. 5:3-5

Lovable Liberator,

You are angry, confused and frustrated. This creates the depression. I allow the surprises to surface, not to confound you with sudden judgments or to harass you, but to train you. Have you heard of "rolling with the punches"? Or "bouncing back"? Or "taking things in stride"? These are the habits I AM teaching you now.

I want you resilient. I want you filled with tough faith. And I want you able to laugh at yourself while still liking yourself. Faith is not idealism. Faith is realism rooted in a settled joy that all things work together for your good.

Today's training is ingraining this conviction. Rejoice and be glad in it! I AM.

Everlastingly,
Your Dad

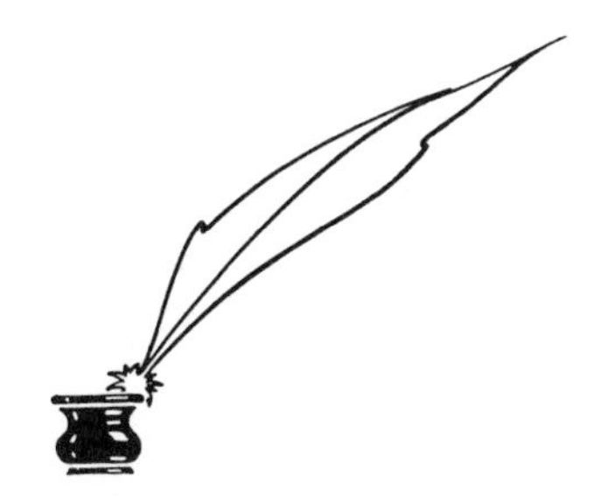

## *A SURRENDERED HEART*

Col. 2:6,7

Son,

A surrendered heart — a heart totally dependent upon My grace — is the greatest gift you can offer Me. I realize your difficulty. You fear the judgment of men. The idea of letting go — of turning loose of your struggles and abandoning your strategies — fills you with panic. "What if 'they' see my lack, my emptiness?" you ask. "What will happen to my testimony, my witness?" I know all your fears.

Son, *think!* Who has promoted you and protected you thus far? Who has covered you, blessed you, given you favor and empowered you? Do you honestly believe I would allow you to be brought to shame? Your own righteousness, your own works pose a greater threat to your public image than your trusting My grace ever has or ever will. But I have covered even these, have I not? Trust Me! Surrender all. Give Me room to act! What have you got to lose? Nothing but your vanity. Thankfully!

Forever in Joy,
Your Dad

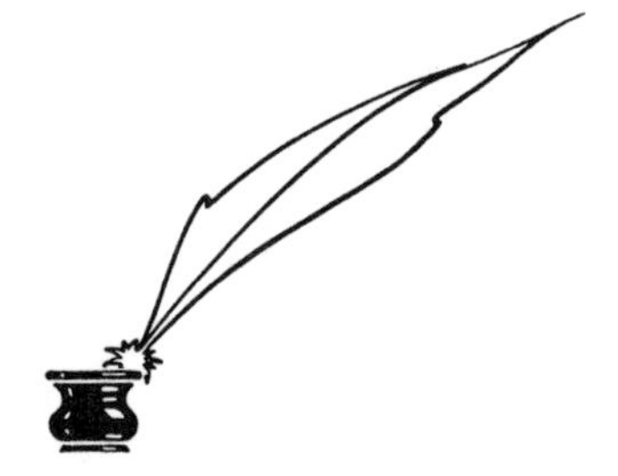

*SIGNIFICANCE*
I Cor. 15:58

Frenzied Fighter,

My ways are not your ways. Again, I AM showing you a path you would have shunned, given the opportunity. And why? I lead you along the road of love — of giving. This road is not a thoroughfare, nor is it a way generally known even among seasoned travelers.

Today I want you to see purpose as I see purpose. Significance is not attached to being seen. In Our Kingdom significance is the outcome of being sent. Your work is not in vain. What you call a waste of time on this mission I call a part of the plan. You would not understand the reason behind it, even if I were to explain it, until you have walked through it. Believe Me! There is no other choice. But you will be glad — soon.

I Promise,
Dad

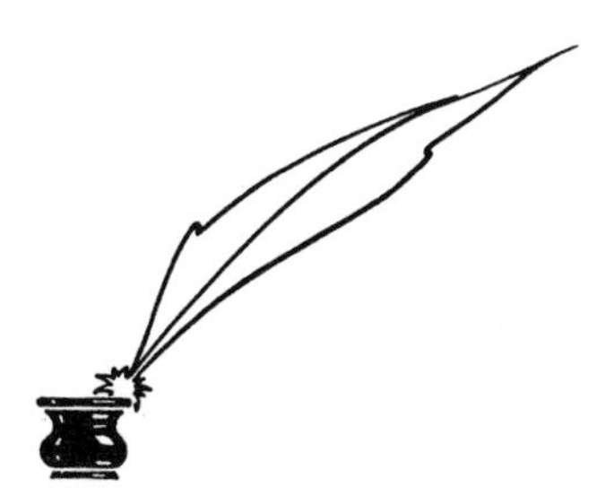

*OPPORTUNITIES*
II Cor. 12:10

Son,

Humble yourself. I didn't say degrade yourself, I said humble yourself. You need faith. You are small; very small indeed. But your present situation is not as difficult as it appears — not if you can see your smallness and My greatness in it. Adopt this perspective and be at peace in this place where I have led you. Here, faith will abound and miracles must multiply. For you will have no one else to depend upon but Me. Not even yourself.

How rarely these opportunities arise at this stage of your walk! But soon you will desire them, not dread them, because the glory of My power shines brightest in the absence of human help.

Always,
Dad

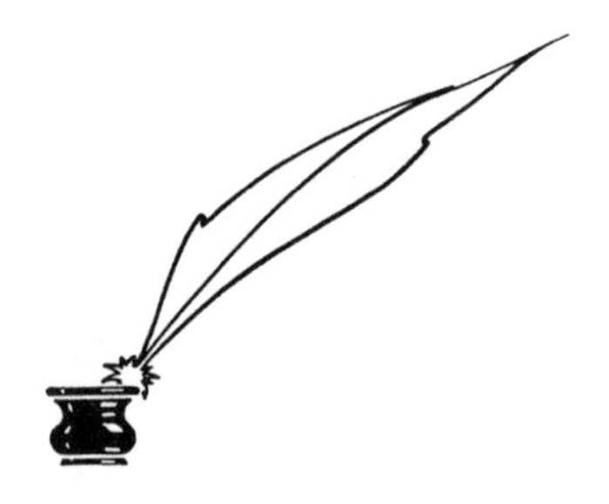

see your
smallness
and my
Greatness
in the situation.
C. Hawkey
©1989

*DELAYS*
Col. 3:15

Frantic Fighter,

Tell Me. Be honest. Do you really have inner peace about this decision? Why do you fear the faces of men? Or the deadlines established by men? Am I not the Master Administrator? Forever, I AM. I AM the Lord of time, and all times are subject to Me.

Has it not occurred to you that the Reason for all the sudden delays speaks to you even now? Why do you complain? Have a sense of adventure! You will like My plans far better than your own — or theirs.

Stop storming about and give no more place to the enemy! Hold fast to the peace I have given you. We All will be grateful if you will.

Love,
Dad

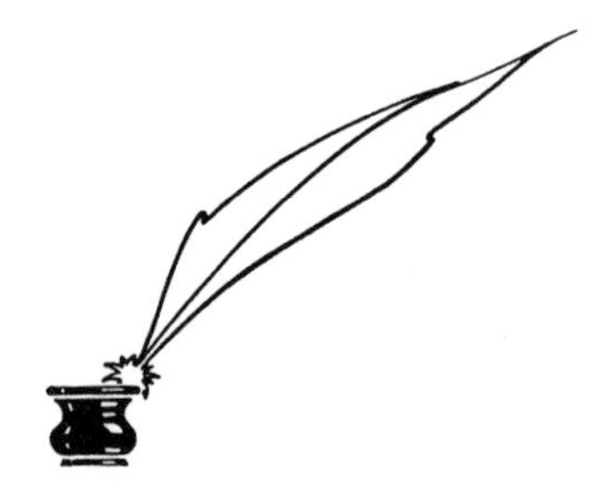

*SEEK TO KNOW ME*
Phil. 3:7-10

Ambitious Conqueror,

Jesus said, "You search the Scriptures, for in them you think you have eternal life, but they are that which testify of Me." So tell Me! Are you searching the Scriptures to learn facts or to learn of Me?

I have called you to friendship, not frenzy. Life, not legalism! Child, seek to know Me, and in knowing Me you will know the truth as well, for truth transcends mere principle in the same way life transcends biological description. The Scriptures will help you to know Me, yes. But only if you meditate upon them with a listening heart. Frankly, I have missed your singing lately...

Love,
Dad

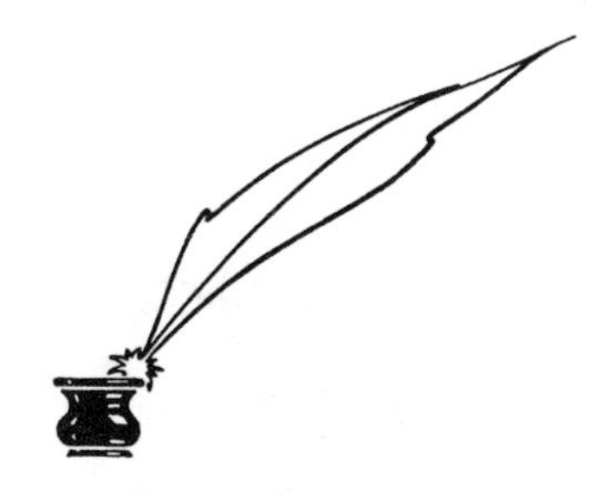

*JOY AND GIVING ARE ONE*
Ps. 127:1,2

usy One,

Has it not yet occurred to you that I AM the One hindering your plans? Or perhaps I should say *saving you* from your plans? Come now! Whose gifts are you seeking to give, yours or Mine? And why?

Consider, little one. Can love and acceptance be bought? No, not in this world or any other. Take it from One who knows — only too well.

Had Jesus given His heart and His life for hurting humanity, expecting love to be returned in kind, then all would have been offered for naught. No, the very act of giving was joy enough.

You are right to believe that joy and giving are one. They are, if the giving finds its origin in My love. But for now, why not allow Me the joy of giving to you? I want to replenish your stores — to enlarge your *capacity* to bless others. Will you stand still long enough to allow Me to do so?

With all My Love,
Dad

*I WILL NOT INTERRUPT*
Isa. 1:18; John 11:6

Little One,

Of course not! I AM not angry with you for questioning. Can Omniscience be offended by any honest pursuit of knowledge? Do you really believe your questions have estranged Us? Never, child! It was I who said, "Come, let Us reason together," was it not?

Now will you wait quietly, giving Me space to answer? Rudeness and haste are contrary to Kingdom policy, so I will not interrupt you. Further, I cannot always conform to your schedule. I love you too much...

Patiently,
Dad

## *CHAPTER OF NEW BEGINNINGS*

I Cor. 15:54,55

Sorrowful One,

Death is forever swallowed up in victory! Receive My strength, child. I AM holding you. Despite the pain, I tell you truly; this is a chapter of new beginnings for you *and* your loved one. I AM mending your heart and you will again know joy.... Yes, unspeakable joy.

You are not wrong to trust Me, so be of good cheer. All will be well. Time and distance are not as your earthly eyes perceive them. Yes, beyond all human hope, and for now in a realm where only I can gain entrance, healing *is* flowing, I promise.

Yes, you will laugh together — again and again — and it will be in My presence that you do so.

Truly,
Father

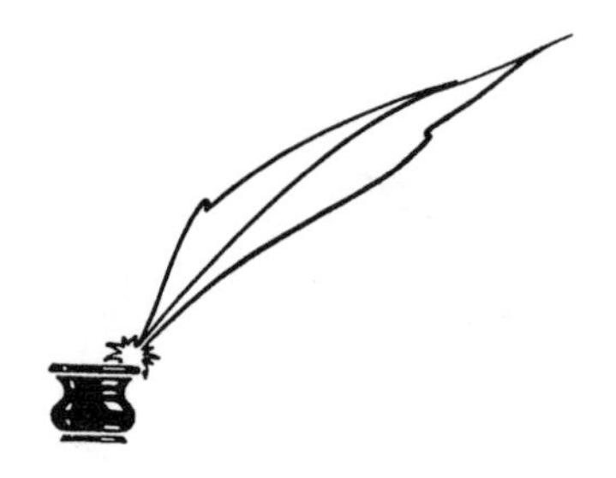

*POCKETS OF PAIN*
Deut. 7:21-23; Heb. 5:8-10

hosen One,

Again, it has been My delight to hold you close, whisper My secrets in your ear, and joy in the wonder of you. I know. There are still some areas We both want to see healed, but those little pockets of pain have been inside you a very long time. And believe it or not, as troublesome as they are, to remove them all at once would be unwise. Through the years, little by little and deep within yourself, you came to think of those inner hurts as part of your identity. As a wise Master Builder I simply know that to replace those faulty parts with the original ones I designed for you does require a certain pace and process.

*Why?* You are always asking why, aren't you? But I have already told you! To heal those inner wounds in a single act of power would deny you the opportunity to grow, to know by experience, and thereby to become a compassionate deliverer. There are some kinds of knowing that only come by growing — otherwise why should My Son have arrived in your world as a baby?

Jesus himself *learned* obedience — sinless though He was — by the things He suffered. Not even He was exempt. To fulfill all righteousness and lay hold of deepest wisdom, even Almighty God had to embrace pain and death. Christ's baptism into suffering and death has become your baptism into glory and life. How so!? HA! Shall I send you a blueprint of the cosmos for starters? The full explanation lies beyond the range of mortal comprehension. At least, such is My view of the matter.

Trust Me! Do you have any other choice?

Tenderly,
Dad

*ALL THE RIGHT THINGS*
I Kings 18:16-39; Matt.18:18,19

hildren,

I know. You did all the right things. You examined your hearts and repented. You exercised your prerogatives of binding and loosing and praying in agreement. You turned your attention away from the difficulty and directed your hearts toward praise — continually. And you were faithful.

So why does the problem remain? Again, as a sovereign witness to My glory, I AM doing the *manifestly* impossible. As My fire fell upon the water-soaked altar at Mount Carmel and consumed the sacrifice, so shall I show My power yet again! Your change *will* come — be assured. But in retrospect, no one will ever be able to ascribe it to natural causes.

Thank you for waiting. Your patience for this witness will be rewarded.

Faithfully,
Father

### *ABRAHAM'S BLESSINGS*
Gen. 21:17-21

Worried Warrior,

Praise is the pathway to peace, as I have told you before. As you rejoice, I redeem; so refuse all rehearsals of past reversals! Did I not bless Ishmael despite the blunders of his father, Abraham? Abraham's blessings are yours, child. Now be at peace.

I AM!
Dad

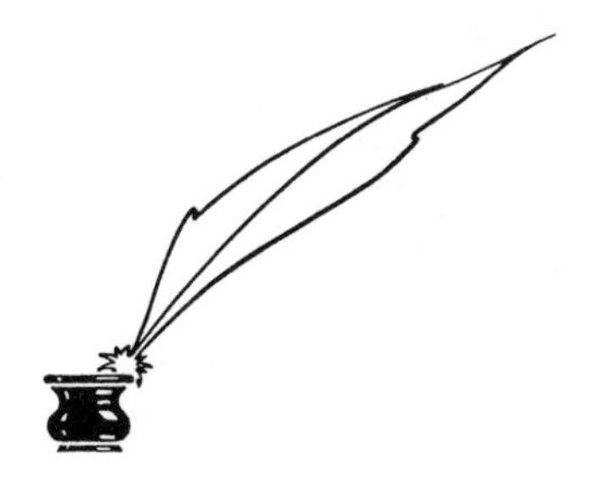

### *YOUR STRONGHOLD OF SECURITY*

Mark 7:26-29; Eph. 3:20

Persistent Seeker,

Are you seeing it now? The whole time you have been bombarding heaven with prayers that seemed to go unanswered, I have been at work. All the while you were questioning, I was quietly healing, restoring and re-arranging.

But you needn't feel guilty over the lashings about of your flesh and your mind that have occurred in this process. Even these have worked for your good; they have deepened your capacity to understand My heart and character.

For instance, you have learned a vital lesson about My sovereignty. Now you are seeing that the phrase "the sovereignty of God" is not an escape clause nullifying My promises. My sovereignty is your stronghold of security! Not only do I fulfill My commitments, but I do exceedingly above and beyond all you ask or think or imagine.

Yes. I do keep you guessing sometimes as to *how* I will answer your prayers — but that is because I AM a Person, not a principle to be manipulated. I AM faithful and reliable, but hardly predictable. Predictability is a characteristic of law and principle, not life and personality. Now you will sing "Great is Thy Faithfulness" and *know* what you are singing about!

How proud of your progress I AM!

Truly,
Father

*THE WINDOWS OF HEAVEN*
Ps. 126; John 15:16

Faithful Children,

Stop reasoning and ask! I have opened the windows of heaven and you need only to ask! Ask and ask largely, for I joy to shower abundance upon you, causing your joy to ignite the faith of your friends.

I told you earlier of the harvest you would reap from those days of sowing in tears, did I not? Then ask. The harvest is ripe, and the day of your freedom has dawned! Stand in agreement with singleness of heart, children, for today is the day of My power. Rejoice and be glad in it!

I AM!
Dad

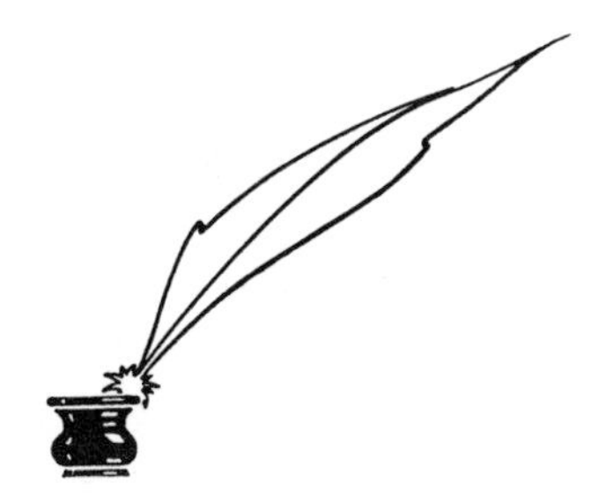

*EXPECTATIONS*
Matt. 5:13; II Cor.10:12; Eph. 2:8-10

hosen Servant,

Why must you worry about the expectations of others? I have called you to be a prototype, not a stereotype — an original, not a copy. Child, you must not even try to fulfill mortal expectations, whether real or imagined! Not only is it a waste of time, it is a disservice to the very ones you would seek to please.

I have called you to be a deliverer — a savior — a champion! If you are to be what I have called you to be, you need to make pleasing *Me* your priority. Will you do that? I AM easier to please than you think, little one. All I ask is that you take time to receive My love, hear My voice, and dare to enact those tactics I share when We come together.

Of course, if you do, you are bound to seem radically different to certain ones at times. How well I know! Yet, if My truth is to be heard and My words are to penetrate, We often will find it necessary to challenge the "norms" of men. Good. If it has to be, then so be it. But be careful — don't start striving to be "different."

Don't seek uniqueness, but neither seek conformity. Seek Me. Always. Inquire of Me and then listen to your heart. I *will* speak and you will know it — and the fruit of your obedience will show it. Peace will permeate your spirit, and quiet confidence will crown all you say and do. As you yield your heart to Mine, your actions will align with Mine, again and again, time after time. Then you will no longer *try* to be bold. No, obedience will *build* you to be bold.

Now will you forsake the futility of your frenzied planning? Be at rest! Be quiet! I AM. Besides, I have already prepared the way.

Your Dad

*EVERY EXTRA MILE*
Gal. 6:9

Delightful Daughter,

To your own eyes your works seem trivial and small, but not to Mine. Every extra mile and every menial task I have carefully noted, and your work has not been in vain.

Thank you for your diligence to help. And thank you for lightening the loads of My other children by doing those mundane details that many would choose to ignore. I have seen every sacrifice, every humiliation and every heartache. You have borne the griefs of many less needy than yourself while suffering pains only I have known. Because you were faithful in small things, I AM choosing you for greater things even now.

Very soon you will enter new joys and the present sorrow will be forgotten. Yes, all that was shattered will be mended and the former things shall be no more. Your labor has *not* been in vain.

Tenderly,
Dad

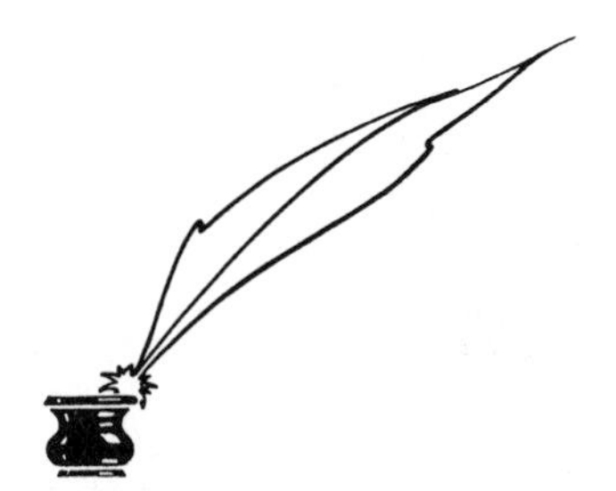

*MY SILENCE*
Ps. 46; Rom. 8:26

uestioning One,

As you know by now, I AM not One to waste words. If, at times, you hear nothing when you seek Me — rest! Abide in the strength of the previous words I have spoken. I often answer on a deeper level than language can express.

Child, in those moments you wait in My presence, what you call My silence is, in reality, My taking the opportunity to infuse you with new life. Every provision, every healing and every solution springs from that quickening. When words are what you need, I will speak them.

Why must We always talk? Stay quiet, restless one! I have longed to hold you...

Gently,
Dad

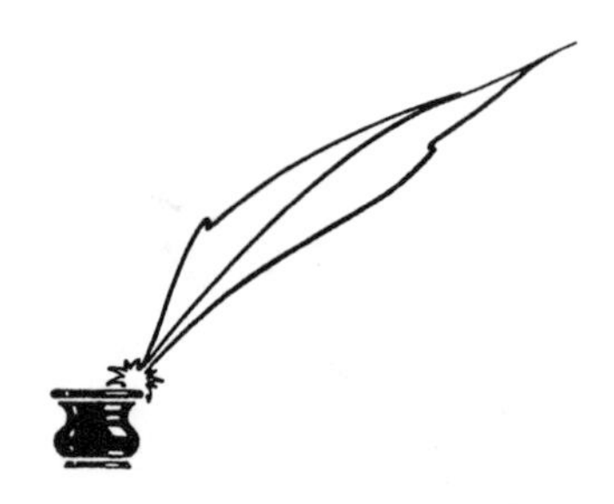

*WHAT DO YOU WANT?*
Prov. 3:5,6

Searching One,

What do you want? Did you not commit your ways to Me? I have seen the surrender of your heart and I AM honoring your request to walk in My will. Move with confidence! There is no chance of your veering off course.

Why do you fear? What you choose *I* will choose! Even if somehow you were to choose a lesser good, you would still be in good hands — hands that are expert in turning smaller goods into greater ones. I AM the Master of time and events, so trust Me! I AM trusting you.

Isn't now as good a time as any for you to taste the joys of Our reigning partnership? I think so. Step out! Be bold. We are destined to succeed, you and I. How could *We* possibly fail?

Committed in Love,
Dad

## *SCRAMBLING THE SIGNALS*

Ps. 107:40-43

Searching Son,

Am I not the Judge above all judges, the Attorney above all attorneys, and the King above all kings? I AM. Again, it is My joy to guard and protect you, and even now I AM scrambling the signals of the opposition. Soon every charge and technicality devised against you will vanish, so sing for joy!

Watch! I AM causing all carnal wisdom to crumble! Soon you will behold the befuddlement of your accusers and stand amazed as I contend with your contenders! Lost in the cloud of their own confusion, your enemies will grope blindly and they each will consume the other. You will see it with your very own eyes. Be assured, you will!

Will the courts of men be caught in the snare of their own craftiness? How could it be otherwise? Corruption can do nothing but invalidate itself, for deceit carries the seed of its own defeat, as I have told you before. Now will you be at peace? I AM.

Always,
Your Dad

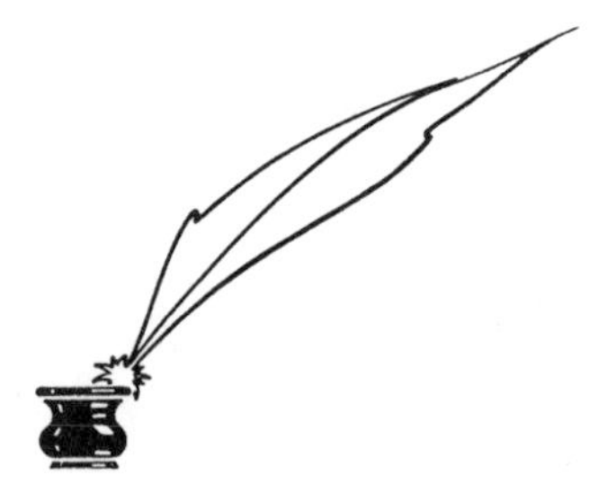

*THE SAME SHARP NEEDLE*
Ps. 18

uestioning Conqueror,

I never promised you a path without resistance or an automatic deliverance which would demand no will or effort on your part. If you'll take a hard look at the life of Jesus you will find it was the same with Him. He *learned* obedience through the things He suffered. In other words, obedience was woven into the fabric of the Son of Man by the same sharp needle of perseverance under pressure which you now encounter.

Think carefully! Do you suppose any prince being trained by his tutors for his future kingship would ever be allowed to bypass basic training? Consider. How would a commander lead an army unless he had experienced the discipline of being a soldier himself? Should a man be made a company president if he has never learned the demands and details of the various departments of the business? Child, I bring this to your attention simply to remind you — the present pressures are not worthy to be compared with the glory I have prepared for you! Trust Me! But trust Me with tenacity and you will come to understand My purposes with conviction and clarity.

Believe Me, if you were unprepared for these things I would have placed you elsewhere. All who would reign with Christ must suffer with Him and undergo discipline to become good soldiers. So be assured; this is practice, not punishment, and you are being prepared for a destiny far higher than you ever dared imagine. Yes, I know. Some of your pain comes from injustice and the failures of anointed leaders in My household. I do understand your disappointment, little one. If anyone understands, I do...

But do you recall the fits of rage and attempted murder My son, David, suffered at the hands of King Saul? And the stress he endured while fleeing for his very life? It was in those times I taught that special man of My heart how to war a good warfare, how to trust only in Me; and it was then that I gave him a gift far greater than ability. I gave him agility. And so it is with you. I AM giving you the feet of a deer that you may tread on the precarious and slippery slopes with ease and delight. One day, glancing back from those exhilarating heights, these present trials will seem trifling in light of the transformation their training produced in you.

Of course, the real design and purpose of the valley through which you have passed *cannot* come into view until you are sufficiently high on the mountains to see with perspective. In the meantime, let Us proceed through the foothills with joy!

Oh? You thought *these* were the mountains? Your tender feet are hardly ready for those yet, little one, but they will be soon enough —*if* you will walk on with Me. Rejoice! I AM giving you beautiful feet — feet fit to run swiftly with the good news of My Kingdom. And I do know what I AM doing! Trust Me.

Always,
Dad

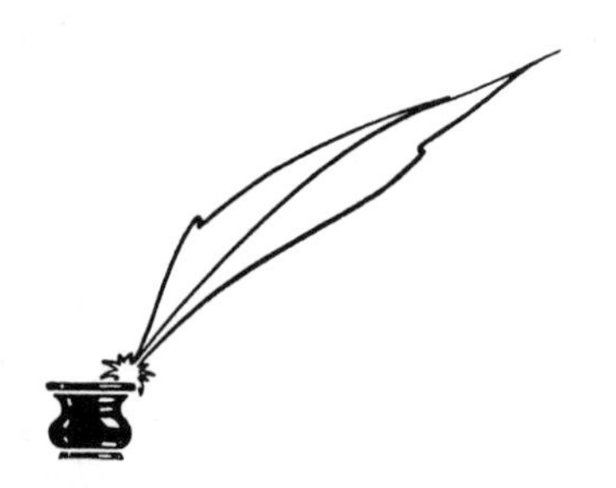

Only until you are sufficiently high on the mountains...
...will the real purpose of the valley come into view.

*GRASPING INGRATITUDE*
Prov. 22:26,27; Matt. 7:6

enerous One,

Yes, I too have been angered by the grasping ingratitude and critical response of your loved ones. And you are right. It seems nothing can please them.

But since you have been so frank in voicing your frustrations of late, I trust you'll not take offense from My being honest with you. *I refuse to take the blame for these events!* No, child, the fault lies with you. And I have protected you more than you know in the midst of your folly. When you gave to them in the first place, why did you not inquire of Me and wait for My answer?

Sometimes I must allow men to come face to face with their lack in order to force them back to reality. Come now! Are you more merciful than I? Have you forgotten what Jesus said about casting your pearls before swine? But never mind. All will be well. Just call it a lesson learned by being burned.

Even so, be sure to forgive. You cannot afford not to. Actually, it was a fairly cheap education — considering all its benefits. Don't you agree?

From now on, seek Me first! If you will, you will find that I empower you to give the very highest gifts. Apart from Me you can do nothing, for only I can assess the truest needs of the heart. There are those times when I give some of My more stubborn children a far greater gift by refusing to yield to their demands. I love them enough to give them room to experience the end of their ways. Have you noticed? Yes, some come to their senses only when mounting expenses compel them at last to seek Me.

I knew you wouldn't mind My rubbing it in a bit...

Cheerfully but Helpfully,
Dad

P.S. But of course I will meet all expenses, child. What are fathers for?

## *UNTIMELY TRUTH*

Rom. 14; Rom. 15:1-13; Col. 2:6-10

Zealous Disciple!

Untimely truth can be just as dangerous as outright error. You can avoid many pitfalls if you will keep this in mind. Think! Do earthly parents teach their children to dance before they have learned to walk? Or should a child of ten be required to learn the same lessons being taught a university student? What would be the use of training an aspiring surgeon in the field of astronomy or teaching ballet to a man preparing for a military career? Child, good educators present a curriculum based upon many factors, including the age, abilities and gifts of their students. Am I not as wise?

Any truth I intend for you will always be timely, helpful and liberating; it will never produce frenzy or despair. Information is not education; ill-timed, it brings disorientation. Will you please trust My timing? Eat only the food I set before you! When in doubt, ask! Wait! If at times some of My more exuberant children share their lessons with you, then you must recognize them as being just that: *their* lessons. And rejoice with them in their new discoveries while remembering this: you are required to fulfill only the assignments I have given to you.

Trust Me. Rejoice in My promises. Enjoy living. And in the simplicity of living you will learn of Me. As I have said, My anointing will teach you all things as you go along.

In Joy!
Your Dad

*THE REAL ISSUES*
Isa. 55:9; II Cor. 4:18

ittle One,

It is no trouble to tell you again; "...as the heavens are higher than the earth, so are My thoughts higher than yours!" You have not been wrong to question. You have just been asking the wrong questions. The enemy always clouds the real issues, don't you remember? Diversion is his oldest trick. But in answer to your question — no. Your present problems are not My punishment, and I have no desire that you suffer for your past sins.

Actually, it is not a matter of *deserving* anything, good or bad. The real issue is the imperishable seed of My Word, for My Word is an inseparable extension of My essence and life. I and My Word are One! So when will you believe in Me? I AM the Seed of Abundant Life and I contain all the fruit you have longed to harvest. But remember, a seed can only sprout if it remains planted. Isn't observing a seed the exact opposite of planting one? Yes, the seed of My Word *must* stay buried in the soil of faith if it is ever to grow.

Keep My Word planted in your heart! Stop looking at outward appearances. Now is the time to decide. Are you going to view this situation through earthly eyes or through the eyes of faith? Is seeing believing? No, little one. Believing is seeing — truly seeing!

If you will stop rationalizing and start rejoicing, you will see what I mean.

Truly,
Dad

### *GROWING UP*

Prov. 3:11,12; I Cor. 13:11,12

Child,

Growing up is never easy. Each new stage of growth from infancy to adulthood requires a weaning from the comfortable and familiar and an embracing of the unknown and the uncharted. And so it is with you.

I cannot always carry you if you are to learn the joy of walking, and neither can I go on spoon-feeding you if you are ever to know how to feed yourself. So, in a sense, you are right. Lately I have "distanced" Myself from you in certain ways so that in more important ways I could bring Us closer together. I do this, not to desert you, but to give you opportunity to grow. In growing, you will discover an intimacy and a closeness between Us which never could have been possible had I dealt with you as I did before. In the same way a full-grown son learns to know the heart of his father far beyond the limited understanding he had as a toddler, so I AM training you to know Me now.

Thus, for a time it will seem as though I AM farther away, but the very reason I created you was that you should join Me in reigning forever! For that to become a reality, you'll have to learn to stand on the two feet I have given you and to trust the spirit I have put within you. Now be honest. Do you think you would put any real effort into learning these things were I to go on hovering over your every move as I did in earlier years? I think we both know the answer to that. Trust Me! I AM trusting you.

Always!<br>
Dad

*I AM FIRMLY COMMITTED*
I John 5:14,15

urious Conqueror,

Far be it from Me to refuse your requests! Have I ever broken My Word? Trust Me, child. I have called you and I will perfect all that concerns you; I AM committed to Our covenant and I *will* perform all I have promised. And yes, you have asked in agreement with My will. No longer question the validity of your petitions. I AM bound by My Word to provide.

Have I not promised that if you ask anything according to My will, you then may rest in the certainty that I have heard you, and you have the things you desired of Me? I remind you — My will is My Word, and My Word is My will. They are one and the same. Therefore, let nothing steal your joy. Even now I AM doing abundantly above and beyond all you have asked or imagined. Late! Since when was *I* ever late?

Confidently,
Dad

*SECRET PROJECTS*
Matt. 6:3,4; John 12:25,26

Faithful Servant,

Even now I AM rewarding you for the long hours you have spent revealing My heart to My needy children. I AM multiplying back to you the gifts you have given. I know. Many have been unthinking where your needs are concerned. Even so, thank you for your willingness to help and comfort them.

Shall I tell you why I sent *you* on this mission? Child, you are one of the few — one of the very few — of My servants willing to work without the guarantee of short-term rewards. Many give readily enough to the destitute, helpless and impoverished. But rarely can I find one willing to love the immature and ungrateful of My children who have not yet learned to give in return. Alas, many of My ministers judge by the outward appearance. They fail to see the desperate poverty beneath the facade worn by those who appear to be more affluent.

Mere decency demands giving to the obviously poor, but who will humble himself to the thankless task of serving the merchants, tax collectors and publicans? You happen to be one of the few, child.

Be prepared. Some will question the abundant gifts I will soon lavish upon you publicly. When they do, just tell them it was My idea, and it had to do with some secret projects We have shared. If they are really troubled about it, I would be more than happy for them to take it up with Me....

Proudly!
Dad

### *TASTE AND SEE*

Zech. 4:6; Matt. 13:16; Col. 2:2,3

Fretful Helper,

Again, you simply must commit your failures and those of all others to Me. Trust Me to finish the work of your salvation — and theirs. Leave all end results to Me. Have you not learned that the flesh is powerless to conquer the flesh? Only by My Spirit can you put to death the deeds of the flesh and live. Not by might, nor by power, but by My *Spirit*! Have you heard?

Think of it this way. A good lawn is more the result of the planting of seeds than the pulling of weeds. It is the same in the heavenly realm. If the good seeds are sown and nourished, they will produce a thick carpet of grass which will choke out most of the weeds.

Here is the working principle: you plant the seeds and I will pull the weeds. Plant them by walking in the joy of My promises! And encourage your loved ones. Today commit yourself to becoming a continuous encourager. *Look* for the praiseworthy! Engender an environment of encouragement. This will release the revelation that only hearts united by love can receive. You then will see the answers to your prayers for your family.

Yes, love them as they are and they will experience the full riches of Christ Himself by walking in the freedom those riches release. In Him alone are contained all the treasures of wisdom and knowledge. Taste and see...

Father

*TIME TO WATER*
Isa. 50:4; Rom. 8:17

uestioning One,

Why do you doubt? Have I ever failed to give you wisdom or direction when you have asked? I have put My words in your mouth and covered you with the shadow of My hand. None of Our words can fail, for My Spirit has anointed your tongue with wisdom to comfort the weary.

There is a time for reaping, but bear in mind that reaping always *follows* the time for planting. Be encouraged! I AM with you. You have not spoken vain or empty words. Allow Me time to water the living Words We have seeded into the hearts of My people. Remember My principle of process — line upon line, precept upon precept, here a little, there a little.

Even Jesus did not always receive immediate results. Often His words were simply rejected. He is your Example, your Teacher; you cannot be greater than He. Rest! If you would share in His ministry, will you not also share in His suffering?

You do not see all. You see only in part, so be of good cheer. You are not called to produce ready-made results. I have called you to bear fruit, and bear it you will, in due time. Your fruit will remain and your harvest will be great. You have My Word about that!

Forever,
Dad

### *REGRETS INTO RESOURCES*

Phil. 3:13-15

Sorrowful One,

About those regrets... Surely you know they are forgiven? It would be wiser now, if you think of them at all, to see them as stepping stones toward knowledge. It is a waste to think of them in any other way, for I turn all regrets into resources.

Have you thought of this? To emphasize your failures is actually to de-emphasize My power! Also, it is to magnify your own significance — especially where the happiness of others is concerned. Child, I alone can bestow happiness for I AM the Source — the very Fountain of Joy! Only insofar as a man chooses to drink from My waters of joy can he be truly happy. And all who do will find their joy full and complete, hardly challenged at all by the flaws and limitations of other mortals.

But understand. This is not to excuse or speak lightly of selfish behavior. Selfish acts are sin and sin cannot be simply excused. It must be forgiven and cleansed by the blood of My Son. Repentance is the only real solution for sin.

But this has not been the need in your case. You sorrow over sins long ago forgiven. The enemy tortures you. He tells you that your sins have caused the griefs and sins of others. It is a lie. For so long I have yearned to comfort you, to give you perspective — a glimpse of it all as I see it. You have not been assigned to assure the happiness of anyone else. You have only one commission, and that is to trust in Me.

Will you choose to trust Me? Remember, trusting, like any other action, is a choice. And while you are making choices, why don't you also decide to make this one — choose to forgive yourself! Self-inflicted punishment can do nothing to alter the past, and continuing remorse is of no value at all. Forgiveness means you are free from your yesterdays — forever! So will you simply enjoy My love again and go on sharing it with others? In this you will fulfill My joy.

And child, thank you for being willing to go the second mile. Well done.

Love,
Dad

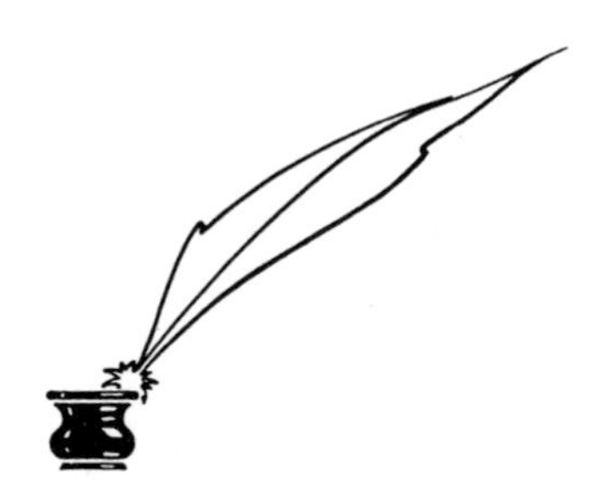

*AN OPEN DOOR*
James 4:13-17; Rev. 3:8

Child,

Surely by now you have learned the folly of forcing a closed door? A forced entry always begets an unhappy ending. Many doors will appear in your lifetime, but not all of them will be yours. And even those that are yours must be entered at the proper time and in the proper way. Any door that would seem to require force should become an occasion for you to inquire of Me. I have set before you an *open* door. Remembering this will spare you further stress.

Cease all remorse and stop trying to analyze your recent blunders. All is forgiven. As I see it, your tenacity is actually one of your more delightful qualities. I simply want to help you put it to better use.

Affectionately,
Dad

## *NO CONFLICT OF INTERESTS*

John 15:1-11

estless Runner,

Why do you fear to open your heart to Me? I have no desire to infringe upon your happiness. What you call "happiness" I call only a clownish copy of joy. Son, I alone can give substance to your hopes, your desires and your dreams — but that is the discovery you have yet to make.

So often you shrink back from Me for fear of loss or unreasonable demands when, in reality, I ask for all of your heart to make possible your having all of Mine. When We each possess the Other's heart, you will clearly see that there can be no conflict of interests...

Love,
Dad

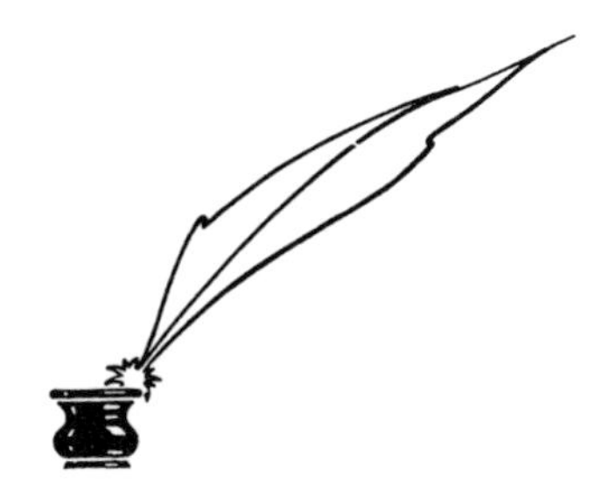

*A NEW MIRACLE*
Isa. 40:31; Luke 18:1-8

aithful One,

The time you spend seeking My face and listening with your heart is never wasted, for though you have never known it, your prayers are as incense before Me. Why do you imagine that I question your love? Your constant return to My Presence surely proves otherwise. Each time you pause to hear My voice, whether you are aware of it or not, a new miracle is seeded within you. Have you not discovered this by now? Rest in this knowledge! The miracle seeded will sprout forth when needed, but let it now take root in the ground. And live one day at a time... Do you really have any choice?

Faithfully,
Father

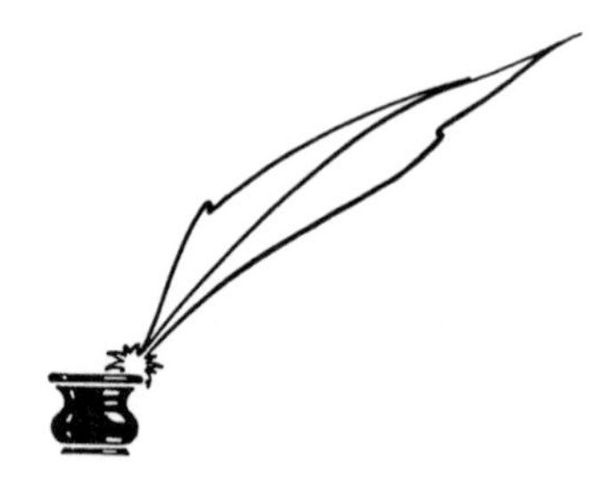

*LOOK ONLY TO ME*
Ps. 25:15

Diligent Daughter,

I repeat. Look only where I instruct you to look, and trust Me to lead you. Learn of Me. Learn the peace that defies reason — the peace that permeated the heart of Jesus. That peace gave Him courage to obey My voice despite the demands pressed upon Him by the family of His dying friend, Lazarus. Lay hold of the bold faith of Elijah, who, in obedience to My word, instructed the widow of Zaraphath to prepare her last morsel of meal to feed him.

I will give you an unearthly calm that no storm, no fiery furnace, and no contradiction can challenge if you will look only to Me. But again — you *must* look only to Me. I will lead you in the way you should go and I will contend with every enemy. Have I not recently told you this? No longer linger between two opinions. Pursue peace, child. I will perfect your path!

With Joy!
Father

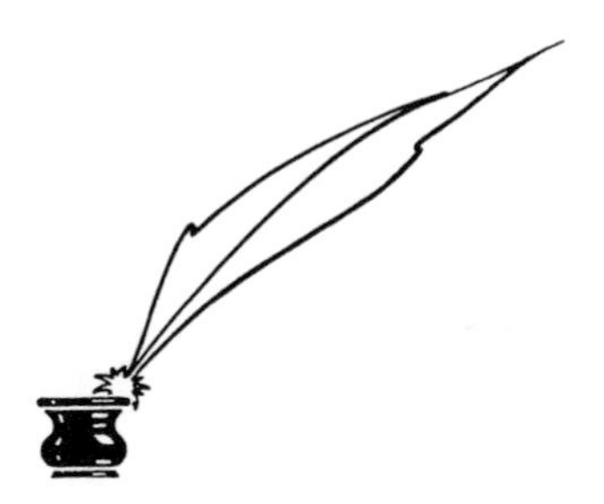

*LET US ENJOY*
Matt. 12:35; I John 4:19

Striving Son,

The law is but a reflection — a verbal description — of the way eternal life *looks* when it is seen in action. This is true of the law of Moses and it is true of the law of Christ, as expressed in the sermon on the mount. So will you please stop *trying* to produce? Apart from Me you can do nothing. Life cannot be produced — it can only be born.

You cannot love your friends, let alone your enemies, unless you are first touched by My love. Did Jesus not say that the good a man speaks comes from the good *stored up* in his heart? Your heart is a tired and empty one. Allow Me to fill it.

And never fear... The radiance of My love from within you will reconcile your enemies or else repel them. Either way, you'll not find them a problem — believe Me.

Father

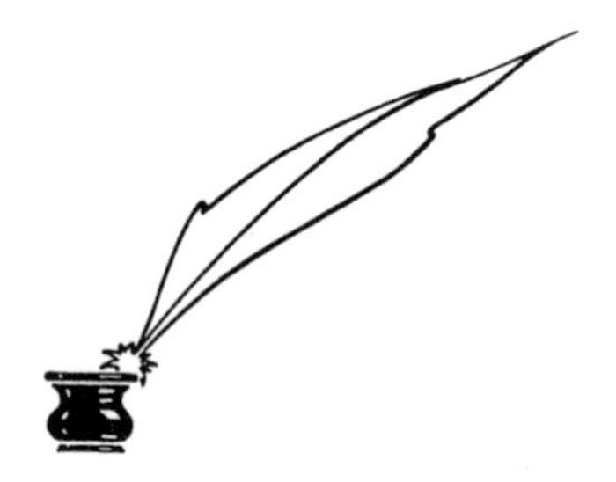

## *CREATED TO CONQUER*

Ps. 91; Phil. 4:6,7; I Thess. 5:24

Struggling Savior,

I really can be trusted. Do you honestly believe I would ignore you in the hour of your greatest need? Peace. I AM arranging events even now to release you from those inner struggles and conflicting demands, and your release will come quite apart from your own strength or striving. This deliverance will not be as stressful as you have imagined, for the worst is already past. Will you rest in Me? The happiness of your loved one is also assured, for I joined you together. You both are covered by My grace.

Why do you imagine yourself unworthy? I have come to the sick, not the well. Child, groveling in remorse will never cure any weakness or produce any good, so shall We leave the past in the past where it belongs?

Cease all introspection, and stop calling yourself names! If you call yourself by the name of a sin, you give it strength by giving it identity. And that is the very thing neither of Us wants. Sin is not your master. I AM. You were *created* to conquer and conquer you will, if you will rest in My love. Remember — Love never fails.

Father

P.S. Soon there will be some interesting provisions coming — seemingly out of nowhere. They will arrive perfectly timed to meet all needs. And there will even be supply for some of your little wants — those secret desires of your heart which I have known, though you have never dared voice them to Me. Pardon My eavesdropping, but being what I AM, it was unavoidable!

### *SHOUTING IN THE HOUSE*
Hab. 2:2-4

Learning Listener,

When will you trust your own ability to hear? Why do you look for fire, thunder and a strange voice resonating from the beyond? Why do you depend upon other listeners?

Trust Me to guide your heart. What do you *think* I *might* be saying in those moments you listen for My voice? When you seek My counsel, choose to heed the words and receive the impressions I give you. Stop attributing them to your own imagination. Why are you surprised that My thoughts "feel" like your own? They are! I gave them to *you*.

Dare to believe! When you ask for a good gift, even if the gift you seek is a word from Me, believe in My integrity. Write down what comes to your mind as you wait before Me. Write the vision and make it as plain as possible. I will confirm all I have said in the hours to follow.

Why don't I speak louder, you ask. Shouting in the house is just not a habit of Mine. Please — allow Me to be Myself with you. Let Me be natural. Shouldn't the Lord of the "supernatural" be the *most* natural of all?

Helpfully,
Dad

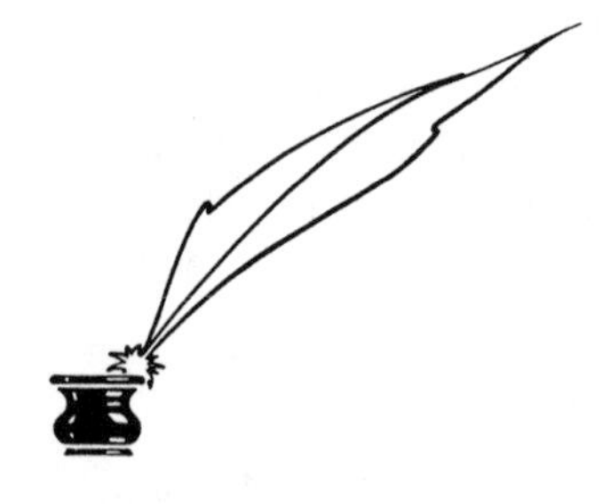

*YOU DESERVE THE BEST*
Eph. 3:20

Child,

All I do, I do in your best interest. In fact, I love you so much that I often look beyond your small requests and give you far better gifts than you ask Me to give. I do supremely above all you ask or think. And why? You are a member of My Royal Family and I think you deserve the best! So will you stop fretting about those "unanswered" prayers? I AM giving you what you really want — not what you think you want. Do you mind?

Cheerfully,
Dad

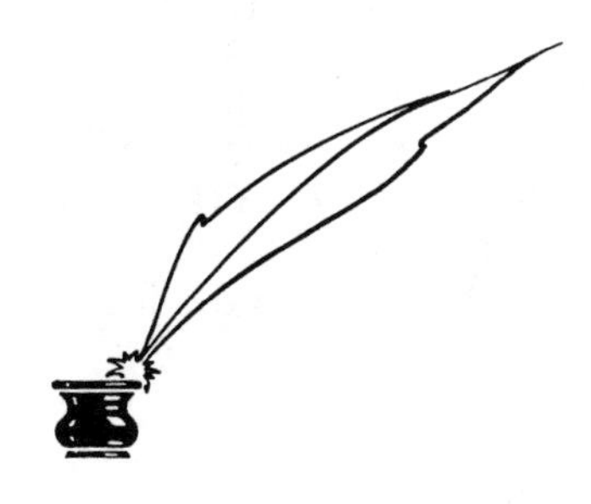

## *THE GREAT ESCAPE*

Eph. 5:14

Bewildered Son,

If there ever should come a time when you feel no further need to grow, beware. Complacency is a fruit of hell, not of holiness. Godliness with contentment is indeed great gain, and no one knows that better than I. Yet may I tell you the vital difference between contentment and complacency? A contented man *cares*, whereas a complacent man *coasts*.

Son, you know I AM the very personification of Perfect Rest, but even I do not coast passively along. I AM unceasingly scanning all creation with searching eyes, *looking* for ways to strengthen needy hearts! Yes, I AM forever in quest to bestow joy upon you and upon all who desire it. And what is joy? Often it is easier to see what a thing is if at first you are told what it is not, so I will put it this way.

Any joy dampening the desire to grow, to go or to give is a delusion and a counterfeit. Any holiness dulling the spirit to the hurts of a dying world is not holiness, but hardness of heart. Any righteousness attained which makes a man feel that at last he is free from the need to lean upon Me will lead to his downfall.

Son, I delivered you once from those dark desires of your earlier years — gladly. But I delivered you, not to parade you about as an advertisement of moral purity or put you on display. I wanted to flood and to energize you with *life*! I longed for the *real* you, the "you" that only Jesus, My Gift of Life, could call forth! The last thing I wanted was a walking, talking "spiritual zombie"...

Now do you see why those old feelings have begun creeping back? The reason they came in the first place was because you walked apart from Me, feeling pressured to become something you could not. Do you remember? Those old fantasies were your only escape.

Repent! Why not take the Great Escape? You've not lost as much ground as you think — I made certain to get you this message before you did.

Love,<br>
Dad

*REVIEW THE STORY*
Gen. 20

Hesitant Warrior,

Wisdom and direction are granted. No longer hesitate, but step out with the confidence of a conqueror. How amazed you will be to see how easily all factors fall into line! You will wonder how you ever could have questioned. Your times are truly in My hands, even as were Sarah's.

Do you recall how I prepared her body for the birth of Isaac by reversing the ravages of time? Sarah, being well-advanced in years, was so obviously restored to her youth that a king once contemplated adding her to his harem, though he did so, much to his court's inconvenience. Review the story for yourself, and remember — the same God is walking with you. Truly, I AM.

Your Father

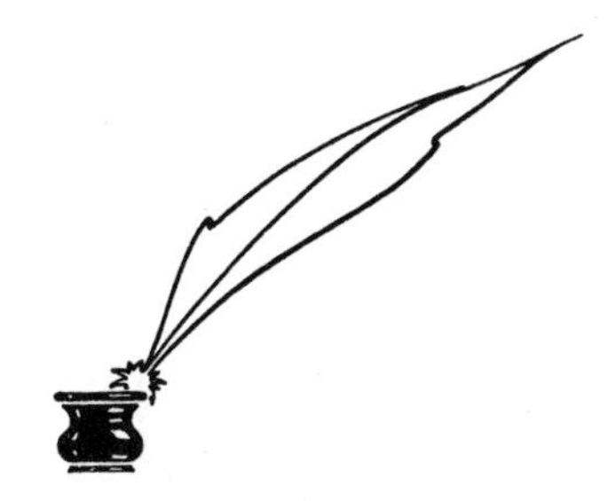

### *TRUST ME FOR YOUR WANTS*
I Sam. 8; Matt. 7:7-11

Frustrated Child,

Why do you keep fretting about those little "wants" of yours? All your life you have feared that I would supply only your bare physical necessities. You have thought My promise to meet all of your needs meant that I would give you nothing else. I ask you! Does a loving earthly father so strictly ration his children?

I know. There are some somber ones who view almost all things as either vain or frivolous. Why do you keep listening to those who think they are more spiritual than I AM!? Things, especially physical things, are neither good nor bad in or of themselves. I've certainly never had a problem with them.

Of course, as a loving and responsible Father, I AM required to withhold from you those things I know would waste your time or bring you pain. For your own sake, I do for you what you would want done — if you but knew all end results. In the meantime, I go on giving you My best gifts. And My best gifts have a quality about them that causes you to grow and mature toward more discerning tastes.

Be patient! Do you remember some of the things you thought you wanted and thought you couldn't live without five years ago? Are you not happy now for their "failure" to materialize? Have you not been glad for My stubbornness? My practicality? My perfect timing?

Israel once longed for a king; being wearied of My government, My people envied to be as other nations. I sorrowed for them. I knew what they desired would bring them far more pain than happiness. Yet, in the end, I granted their request, for they could learn no other way. And since having an earthly kingdom was better than having none at all, I gave them the kingdom they thought they wanted. But they could have had Mine...

Will you learn from them? I desire a more excellent

way for you. Receive My greater gifts. Trust Me! You will see that I do have all your interests and happiness at heart.

In fact, within these next few weeks and even in the next seven days, you will see Me provide — in microscopic detail — many of those little wants you have expressed. By the way, you are in for some surprises. You have forgotten that you even asked for some of the things you are about to receive. You forgot, but I did not.

Haven't I shown you that you need not always ask Me directly? That I delight to surprise you with the little things? Things which you mention to others or just simply wish? You know I have.

Soon you will be older and know Me better and then you will strive angrily against Me less. You have exhausted yourself with shadow-boxing, child. I AM not against you. I AM for you!

How I long for the day when you discover how much I greatly delight in you...

Always,
Dad

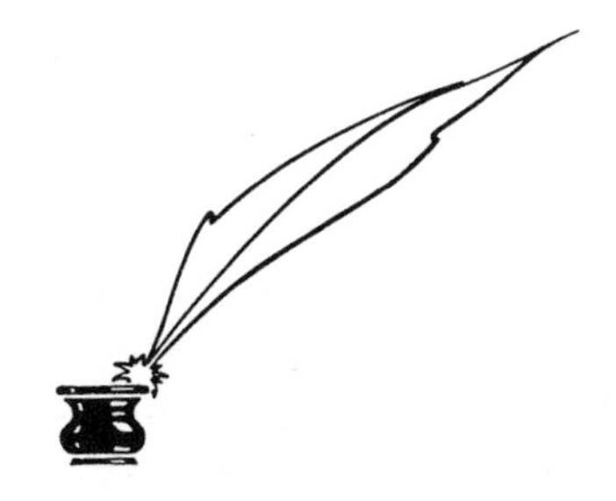

*MAGIC SHOW?*
Ezek. 33:30-33; John 6:26,27

Child,

When you seek Me for guidance, do you delight in the "revelation" I give you more than you delight in Me? Is your joy more rooted in the fact that I have spoken than in living out and putting into practice what you have heard Me say? This is a common trap and I want you to be aware of it.

This is why I have lately withheld My revelations — My supernatural acts. I have longed that you would love Me more than you love the loaves and the fishes I miraculously multiply. When you started *storing* the bread instead of eating it, when you began *analyzing* the fishes instead of cooking them, I had no choice. I had to call a halt to the "supernatural." Had I gone on showering miracles and manifesting My power, I would have been conducting a mere magic show — a performance to be connoisseured and critiqued! I have better things to do.

I AM sorry — for both of Us. My heart aches for your pain, but also for the loss of your love. Have I not proven Myself? When will you learn to love *Me*?

Entreatingly,
Father

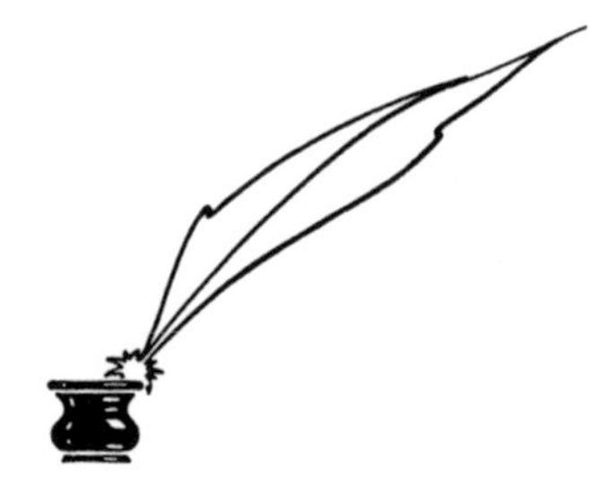

*ON THE RIGHT TRACK*
Ps. 31:14-16; Matt. 6:33,34

Busy Daughter,

I know it seems a senseless waste of time to wait quietly before Me when there is so much to be done — especially for an active "doer" like yourself. I AM also aware of the struggles you have with guilt feelings when you do set aside those quiet moments to hear My voice.

Isn't it interesting how the enemy suddenly starts harping about "practicality" and "the need for good time management" when you are taking time for Us? Amazing! Little one, if you have him worried, you must be on the right track! Stop worrying and keep enjoying Our fellowship. Spending time with Me has already saved you far more time than you think. But your own recent experience has proven this already — has it not?

Truly!
Dad

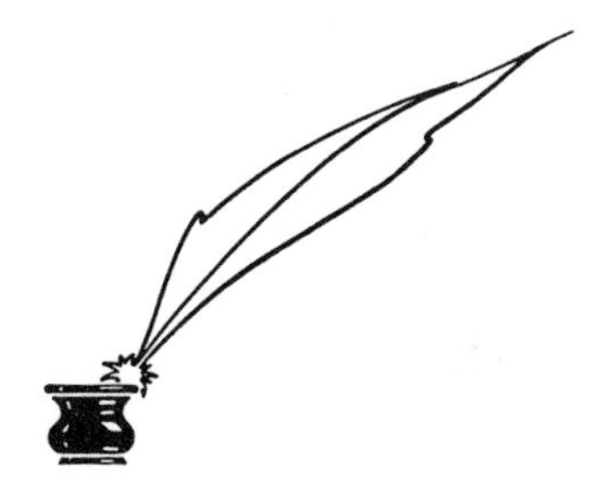

*KINGDOM WISDOM*
Eccl. 11:1; II Cor. 4:15-18

Faithful Conqueror,

Now do you see it? Everything, literally *everything* you commit to My trust is redeemed and returned to you multiplied! It was hard going there for awhile, but reaching the end of yourself did put you in reach of Something greater, did it not?

Obedience is better than sacrifice, as the recent restorations obviously show. Yes, trusting your loved ones to Me, you will be happier with the outcome — always. Remember, Kingdom wisdom never worries and mountains are moved by Mercy, not manipulation. Will you teach this to the children?

Thanks Again!
Father

*WHAT HAVE YOU GOT TO LOSE?*
I Cor. 2:7-16; I Cor. 6:17

Courageous Conqueror,

I AM for you, I AM with you, and I AM in you. You have heard My words, beheld My acts of deliverance, and seen My wisdom at work repeatedly. My power rests upon you and the mind of Christ saturates your spirit.

So why are you seeking mere scraps of information again? My character and heart have permeated your own more than you have dared to believe. I repeat! Speak and you will see — go and you will know!

Stop depending on formulas and regulations! Use the eyes of your heart. Dare to say and do what you see Me saying and doing. Do what you *believe* Jesus would do were He doing it Himself! Then you will discover that He *is* — through you. *Put on* the mind of Christ! Then do as He did. Start speaking words that sound like Mine and start taking steps that look like Mine, and you will find all your acts *will* be Mine, I promise. What have you got to lose? I think we've both noticed you're not very good at rule keeping...

Honestly but Affectionately,
Dad

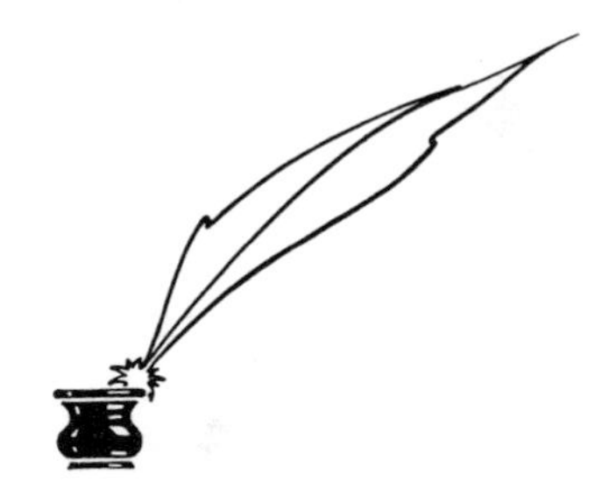

*GO IN PEACE*
Eph. 1:5,6

Children,

Go in peace. Every appointment I have planned for your joy. Every encounter, every transaction, and every move I have foreseen and established for your blessing. And why have I chosen you? Will it satisfy you if I tell you I did it because I *wanted* to?

I AM in control, so refuse to fear! Your faith will bring its own rewards and you will lack no good thing; neither will you owe any man anything — except the debt of love.

Truly,
Dad

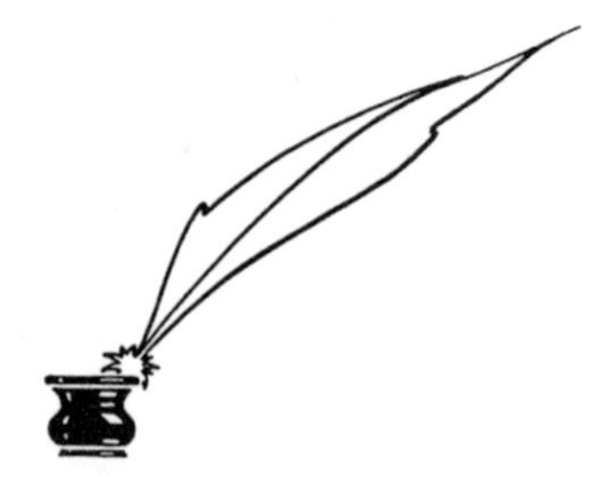

# Postscript

Do you know your heavenly Father — personally? Or do you just know about Him? Have you ever heard Him chuckle, or congratulate you or tell you He loves you? Has He ever comforted you, or given you miraculous and sudden bursts of insight — revealing knowledge otherwise unobtainable? Do you have conversations with your heavenly Father? Do you ask Him questions? Do you hear Him telling you "yes" or "no," or giving you timely words of counsel? Have you come to know Him as a warm, loving, all-wise and all-powerful "Dad"? The Bible teaches that our Father really wants each of us to know Him in that way.

The Bible is God's perfect love letter to us. He sent us that love letter to lead us to Jesus Christ, our Father's greatest Gift to our world. And Jesus came to show us His Father and to *demonstrate* how we should relate to Him. He literally conversed with His Father all the time! Jesus knew the Scriptures, but He also knew the God of the Scriptures — intimately. Christ used the eyes and ears of His heart and was led by the Holy Spirit. He declared that He did only what He "saw" His Father doing and spoke only what He "heard" His Father saying. And here is the real shock: Jesus told *us* to do as He did! In fact, He created us to enjoy *real* conversations with the *real* and *living* God.

When you think about it, the whole reason Jesus came, lived, died and rose again was to make possible that kind of relationship with our Dad. Christ wants us to be walking, talking miracle-workers who hear the voice of our Father and enact His tactics to liberate hurting people. We have been chosen to be co-rulers with Almighty God — forever!

It all begins now, but planet Earth is only our training ground.

Sound incredible? It is! The mere thought of our destiny is so awesome, it jolts our limited intelligence systems into "thermal overload." Our call is too grand and too vast for our small minds to compute; but it is true.

If all this sounds foreign to you, too far-flung, but somehow strangely captivating, I invite you to join me in the following prayer. Pray it aloud:

> "Heavenly Father, I want to know You in a real way — a personal way — just like Jesus did. I realize that You sent Your only Son, Jesus Christ, into this world to make that possible. He died on the cross for my sins and was raised to life by the power of Your Spirit. Now I commit all that I am to Jesus' care — to His Lordship. Your Word says that if I confess Jesus as Lord, I will become Your child, Your heir. I decide now to believe that promise and receive Jesus as my Lord.
>
> Thank You for honoring Your Word and adopting me into Your family. I know I can trust You. And Father, please lead me to some of Your older children. Send me among men and women who already talk to You and hear You talking to them. I want to learn from them. Protect me from those who are "religious" but deny Your power to speak today, and keep me from any other influence that would hinder my relationship with You.
>
> In Jesus' name, Amen.

Take this opportunity to affirm this life-changing transaction by your own written testimony:

On this ____ day of __________, in the year of our Lord ______, I, ______________________________, entered into a covenant relationship with my heavenly Father. I yielded my life to the Lordship of Jesus Christ, and by the promise of my loving Father, I now belong to Him forever. I hereby consent for my God to exercise His full parental prerogatives on my behalf. Henceforth I will look to Him to be my Dad and will trust Him to keep my tomorrows.

(signed) ______________________________

## Scriptures to strengthen your faith:

| | |
|---|---|
| John 1:12, 3:16 | God promises eternal life. |
| John 5:39 | The Scriptures lead us to Christ. |
| John 5:19,30 | Christ hears the voice of His Father. |
| John 14:12 | We, too, can hear our Father's voice. |
| Isaiah 55:1-3,10,11 | Our Father longs to commune with us. |
| Matthew 7:7-11 | Our Father will talk to us if we ask. |
| James 1:5 | Our Father will give us His wisdom. |
| Romans 8:14,15 | Abba Father is the name for Dad. |
| Romans 8:16,17 | We reign as co-heirs with Jesus. |
| John 20:21 | Jesus commands us to be miracle-workers, too. |

# Index

Have the letters from this book helped to fortify your faith or given you needed encouragement? If so, you will **definitely** enjoy the cassette!

Through this anointed cassette, Paula and Charles share selected excerpts from the book 'From the Father's Heart.' Rendered in a warm and natural manner, this dramatic presentation is packed with powerful insight. It is prayerfully tailor-made to aid in your own private devotions!

The innovative orchestration of Flech Wiley in the background will lift you into joy, and the words you hear will saturate your spirit with strength. You will sometimes chuckle, and you will often be inspired to weep—or worship. This tape is an invitation to intimacy with the DAD above all Dads... Father God Himself.

If you think you would like to order this cassette or more copies of this book, 'From the Father's Heart,' please fill out the order form on the following page and send it to the appropriate address.

Charles and Paula Slagle minister to hundreds of people all over the world by a bi-monthly cassette as well as a **monthly** ministry letter.

Many times the Slagles read their latest "letters" (not yet published) on this tape. They also often print them in their monthly letter of ministry—as the Lord leads. Through this monthly correspondence they teach and share prophetic messages to strengthen their financial partners and give news of their travels.

If you desire to partner with Charles and Paula in publishing the good news by providing monthly financial support and receive their monthly ministry correspondence, please fill out the order form on the following page and send it to the appropriate address.

## *Tape and Book Collection/United Kingdom*

If local bookstores do not stock these items, use this order form.

| Quality | Description | Cost | Total |
|---|---|---|---|
| | *From the Father's Heart* Book | £5.50 | |
| | *From the Father's Heart* Cassette | £6.50 | |
| | *Power to Soar* Book | £2.95 | |
| | **Shipping: add 10% of total order** | **Shipping** | |
| | **or £2.00, whichever is higher.** | **Total** | |

**NOTE**: Any orders shipped to other than U.K. add £2.00 per item. CASH CAN GET LOST IN THE MAIL! Send Check or Money Order payable to:

**Charles and Paula Slagle Min., Inc.**
**P.O. Box 31**
**Romford, Essex RM6 4JB**

**NOTE:** Please print clearly.

Name ________________________________________

Address ________________________________________

________________________________________________

## *Special Monthly Message*

God has spoken to my heart to financially support your ministry monthly. I also would like to receive your monthly ministry correspondence. I understand that £4 monthly will only meet the expense of your materials, labour, and mailing costs. But I desire to help increase your ministry, so my monthly offering will be:

❑ £5 ❑ £10 ❑ £25 ❑ £50 ❑ Other $____________.

POWER
to Soar
New Strength Daily
from the Father's Heart
CHARLES SLAGLE

IMAGE
digest